EARLY
IN THE
MORNING

BOOK 2

To Ken, with love,
Sharon
Christmas 1990

EARLY IN THE MORNING

BOOK 2

WOODROW MICHAEL KROLL

LOIZEAUX BROTHERS
Neptune, New Jersey

EARLY IN THE MORNING, BOOK TWO
© 1990 by Woodrow Michael Kroll.

A publication of Loizeaux Brothers, Inc.
A nonprofit organization devoted to the Lord's work and to the spread of His truth

All Scripture quotations have been taken from the Authorized King James Version.
Italics have been added by the author for emphasis.

Printed in the United States of America

Library of Congress Cataloging-in-Publication Data
(Revised for volume 2)

Kroll, Woodrow Michael, 1944-
    Early in the morning.

    1. Meditations.   I. Title.
BV4832.2.K75 1986   242'.5   86-10572
ISBN 0-87213-474-1 (v. 1)
ISBN 0-87213-477-6 (v. 2)

Dedicated to
all my students
who have had to rise

Early in the Morning

to attend my classes

Contents

Devotional Title	Morning Verse	Page
GOD'S PERFECT WILL	1 Samuel 9:26	10
PARTNERSHIP	Genesis 31:55	12
REFORMATION	2 Chronicles 29:20	14
GOD'S UNFAILING WORD	Luke 21:38	16
EFFECTIVE PRAYER	2 Kings 19:35	18
OUR MAJESTIC GOD	Exodus 19:16	20
MORNING MERCIES	Lamentations 3:22-23	22
A LONG DAY	Acts 28:23	24
GOD'S ABIDING PRESENCE	1 Samuel 11:11	26
YIELDING TO GOD	Genesis 32:24	28
PERFECT PROMISES	Joshua 6:15	30
FRIENDSHIP	2 Samuel 17:22	32
AWAKE EARLY	Psalm 108:2	34
FLEECE OR FAITH	Judges 6:38	36
INCOMPLETE OBEDIENCE	1 Samuel 15:12	38
PRAYER AND PEACE	Isaiah 26:9	40
REASONABLE SERVICE	Exodus 24:4	42
THE GIFT OF CRITICISM	John 8:2	44
GLORY TO GOD	Judges 7:1	46
MORNING MOMENTS	Psalm 119:147	48
COME AND DINE	John 21:4	50
LITTLE THINGS	1 Samuel 17:20	52
PRAISING GOD	1 Chronicles 23:30	54
BELIEVING IS NOT SEEING	Isaiah 37:36	56
JOY IN THE MORNING	Psalm 30:5	58
WEB OF CONSPIRACY	Judges 9:33	60
GOD ALONE	Job 7:4	62
FAILURE AND SUCCESS	Joshua 8:10	64
THE DECEITFUL HEART	Exodus 32:6	66
REWARDABLE SERVICE	Matthew 20:1	68
JEALOUSY	1 Samuel 20:35	70
FIRM IN FAITH	Mark 16:2	72
CHARACTER	Psalm 73:14	74
BETRAYAL	Judges 16:2	76
FOOLISH VOWS	Genesis 44:3	78
MYSTERIOUS WAYS	Numbers 22:13	80

THE TRIAL OF FAITH . . . .   Job 24:14   82
MORNING MARCHING ORDERS . . . .   Psalm 143:8   84
VENGEANCE . . . .   1 Samuel 25:36   86
HOSPITALITY AND INHOSPITALITY . . .   Judges 19:5   88
HIDDEN RESOURCES . . . .   2 Samuel 23:4   90
GOD'S PROVIDENCE . . . .   1 Samuel 29:10   92
MORNING PRAISE . . . .   Psalm 113:3   94
HE IS ALIVE . . . .   Mark 16:9   96
PRIDE . . . .   2 Samuel 24:11   98
RELYING ON GOD . . . .   Psalm 127:2 100
JESUS FIRST . . . .   Revelation 22:16 102
STANDING TALL . . . .   Job 1:5 104
INGREDIENTS FOR SERVICE . . . .   Exodus 34:2 106
THE HIDDEN HAMMER . . . .   Job 7:21 108

Preface

ALTHOUGH there are twenty-four hours in each day, some of those hours are more glorious than others. By far the freshest hours of the day for me, and the most productive, are those that precede the glistening rays of the morning sun. It is then that I meet the Commander-in-Chief and get my marching orders for the day. If I fail to meet Him first, I usually fail to meet Him entirely.

An unknown poet expressed it this way:

> A moment in the morning—
>   a moment, if no more—
> Is better than an hour
>   when the trying day is o'er.
>
> 'Tis the gentle dew from heaven,
>   the manna for the day;
> If you fail to gather early—
>   alas! It melts away.

God does things "early in the morning." Each of these devotional stories centers on a biblical event that occurred at the dawning of the day. It is my prayer that by meditating "early in the morning" on these early morning events each of us will walk more closely with the Lord throughout the day. After all, if we do not begin the day with Him, how can we spend the day with Him?

God's Perfect Will

MORNING SCRIPTURE   1 Samuel 9:15–10:1
MORNING VERSE   1 Samuel 9:26

And they arose early: and it came to pass about the spring of the day, that Samuel called Saul to the top of the house, saying, Up, that I may send thee away. And Saul arose, and they went out both of them, he and Samuel, abroad.

S AMUEL had been a judge for many years and was yielding to advanced age. Who would lead the people after his death? Like the sons of Eli before him, both of Samuel's sons, Joel and Abiah, had disqualified themselves for they had "turned aside after lucre, and took bribes, and perverted judgment" (1 Samuel 8:3). If Israel did not choose a king and Samuel died, anarchy would once again prevail as it had in the days of the judges, when everyone did "that which was right in his own eyes" (Judges 17:6).

Besides, without a king Israel was missing out on all the pomp and ceremony that the other royal courts of the ancient Near East enjoyed. While the Jews were wandering nomads, unsettled and without a homeland, they cared little about what other nations did or had. But now they had become firmly established in the promised land and all the surrounding nations had a king. Why not Israel?

In the permissive will of God, Saul was to be that king. The son of Kish, a wealthy and influential Benjamite, Saul as choice for king may appear to the untrained eye as a matter of pure chance. Sent by his father to round up some stray donkeys and failing to locate them, Saul decided to appeal to Samuel the prophet for assistance in locating the strays. The day before God had forewarned Samuel that on the morrow a Benjamite, whom he should anoint to be captain over Israel, would approach him. When Saul arrived there was little question in the priest's mind about his identity. Blessed with natural graces and talents, not to mention that he was head and shoulders taller than any of the other Jews, Saul was the natural selection for king of Israel. But more than this, in the permissive will of God, his was also the supernatural selection. Jehovah had decided to give Israel her wish, for better or for worse, and Saul was His selection for the man who would be king.

As the Benjamite approached Samuel the word of Jehovah came to the priest and he said, "Behold the man." Led to the banquet chamber of the high place, Saul and his servant were seated above the thirty guests who had assembled there. Samuel instructed the cook to bring the best portion of the meat from the sacrifice and place it before Saul. More than this, something that is rarely done, Samuel invited Saul to stay with him that night and sleep upon the top of the house. *They arose early* after communing through the night and made their way through the city where Samuel took a vial of oil, poured it upon Saul's head, gave him the kiss of homage, and anointed him as captain over the Lord's inheritance, the nation Israel (1 Samuel 9:26).

To live in God's permissive will is but to receive temporary blessing. Saul is one of the great tragic figures of Old Testament history. Although selected by God at the cries of the people, he degenerated into a psychopathic condition in which his powers were sapped and his kingdom was rent from his hands. Rejection, defeat, and suicide were the inevitable results.

Perhaps a mere coincidence, it is nonetheless striking that when the priest encountered the man who in God's permissive will would become king of the Jews he said, "Behold the man" (1 Samuel 9:17). Centuries later when Pilate encountered the man who in God's perfect will would become King of the Jews, he likewise said, "Behold the man!" (John 19:5). Saul's reign was immediately accepted by the people because he was handsome and they anticipated he would lead Israel successfully into battle against her enemies. Jesus' reign was immediately rejected by the people for He had "no form nor comeliness" and He never intended to lead His people victoriously against Israel's enemy. Saul was Israel's choice; Jesus is God's choice. How much better off we are to live in His perfect will rather than to settle for His permissive will.

MORNING HYMN

> *Simply trusting ev'ry day,*
> *Trusting through a stormy way;*
> *Even when my faith is small,*
> *Trusting Jesus that is all.*

Partnership

MORNING SCRIPTURE   *Genesis 31:17-55*
MORNING VERSE   *Genesis 31:55*

And early in the morning Laban rose up, and kissed his sons and his daughters, and blessed them: and Laban departed, and returned unto his place.

THE LORD watch between me and thee, when we are absent one from another" (Genesis 31:49). How frequently these words are used as a benediction, especially at the close of a church service. They seem to express the prayer of two parties for mutual protection by the Lord until such time as they are safely and happily reunited. However, the context in which these words were uttered compels just the opposite conclusion.

Jacob was a scoundrel. He took advantage of his twin brother Esau by persuading him to sell the birthright for a mess of pottage. Later Jacob lied to his father and tricked Isaac into bestowing on him the irrevocable family blessing. Even Jacob's name means "supplanter, one who removes or replaces by scheming or treachery." Yet he met his match in father-in-law Laban. When Jacob reached Haran he spied the beautiful Rachel and agreed to serve Laban seven years for her hand in marriage. At the end of those seven long years Laban tricked Jacob by switching his daughter Leah for Rachel. This meant another seven years of labor for the girl Jacob loved. In all, the patriarch served fourteen years for Laban's daughters and six years for a herd of cattle.

At the end of this time God reminded Jacob of the vow he made to return to the promised land. Jacob asked Laban to release him and permit his return to Bethel. This, however, would have ruined Laban financially. Scoundrel that he was, Jacob was still heir to the promise of God and Laban knew that the secret of his own increasing wealth was God's blessing on Jacob. Therefore Laban proposed that Jacob forget about leaving and become his partner. This meant that Jacob's only recourse was to depart secretly from Haran while Laban was away shearing his sheep.

Aware that she would receive no inheritance from her father, Rachel removed the family gods as she prepared to leave Laban's house. Archaeological excavations at Nuzi in northern

Mesopotamia indicate that when the household gods (teraphim) were in the possession of a son-in-law, he was legally designated as the principal heir. For this reason Rachel stole her father's gods without the consent or knowledge of Jacob.

When Laban learned of his son-in-law's hasty departure he pursued Jacob and his family. Seven days later at Mount Gilead Laban overtook them and immediately confronted Jacob about the stolen gods. Having no knowledge of them, Jacob permitted a search to be made. The gods, cleverly hidden by Rachel, were not found and this only served to increase the distrust between father and son-in-law. It was obvious that the suspicion between the two could not continue indefinitely. Therefore a covenant was devised which would not permit either party to further impede the other. Sworn to at Mizpah, the terms of the covenant were simple. A pile of stones was erected as a heap of witness between Laban and Jacob that from that day forward neither one would pass beyond that heap in order to do the other harm. Since the only witness to this event was God, the two men said, "The LORD watch between me and thee, when we are absent one from another." Suspicion and distrust are clearly present in this malediction. *"Early in the morning* Laban rose up, and kissed his sons and his daughters, and blessed them,"* returning to Haran (Genesis 31:55). He is never heard from again in the narrative of Scripture.

Jacob, the man of God, had made a covenant with Laban, the man of the world. The Bible does not prohibit God's children from making necessary pacts with the world. Frequently such business covenants or contracts are made. However, the Bible does warn against making unequal partnerships or yokes with the world (2 Corinthians 6:14). For twenty years Jacob carefully eluded making such a yoke with Laban even though he was his father-in-law. The man of God knew that a lifetime with the world, enticing and profitable as it may have seemed, was no substitute for the blessings of the promised land. Christians today still need to learn that lesson.

MORNING HYMN

> *I am resolved no longer to linger,*
> *Charmed by the world's delight;*
> *Things that are higher, things that are nobler,*
> *These have allured my sight.*

Reformation

MORNING SCRIPTURE   2 *Chronicles 29:20–30:12*
MORNING VERSE   2 *Chronicles 29:20*

Then Hezekiah, the king, rose early, and gathered the rulers of the city, and went up to the house of the LORD.

U NLIKE the ten northern tribes of Israel, which had only downs, the two tribes of Judah to the south had their ups and downs. Just five or six years before the northern kingdom came to an end with the fall of Samaria, Hezekiah became king of Judah. As the thirteenth king of Judah, Hezekiah succeeded his father Ahaz in the third year of Hoshea, the nineteenth and last king of Israel. He was twenty-five years old when he began to reign and had a long reign of twenty-nine years in Jerusalem.

In contrast to his father, Hezekiah proved to be the most faithful to Jehovah of any of Judah's kings since David. It is said of him, "And he did that which was right in the sight of the LORD, according to all that David his father had done" (2 Chronicles 29:2). Ben Sira, the ancient historian, reckons Hezekiah with David and Josiah as the only three kings who did not forsake the law of the Most High God. Of him it is written, "He trusted in the LORD God of Israel; so that after him was none like him among all the kings of Judah, nor any that were before him. For he clave to the LORD and departed not from following Him, but kept His commandments which the LORD commanded Moses. And the LORD was with him; and he prospered whithersoever he went forth" (2 Kings 18:5-7).

In the very first month of his reign, Hezekiah set in motion the most thorough religious revival that Judah had ever known. This revival began by reopening and repairing the doors of the Temple which had been closed by Ahaz, and by cleansing and purifying that sacred edifice. Undoubtedly the prophet Isaiah had a beneficial influence on Hezekiah to initiate such a revival. There is even a Jewish tradition that he was a cousin of King Hezekiah. Regardless, he is said to have prophesied in the reign of four kings of Judah: Uzziah, Jotham, Ahaz, Hezekiah (Isaiah 1:1). Together, Isaiah as prophet and Hezekiah as king, they would restore the religion of Israel to the worship of Jehovah.

In just eight days the house of the Lord was restored and sanctified. The report came back to Hezekiah that the priests and Levites had cleansed the house and the altar of burnt offerings with all the vessels and the table of shewbread thereof. These had been discarded during the reign of Ahaz.

After all had been made ready, "Hezekiah the king *rose early*, and gathered the rulers of the city, and went up to the house of the LORD" (2 Chronicles 29:20). The priests made the appropriate sacrifices and the Levites with cymbals, psalteries, and harps began to praise the Lord with music. All the congregation worshiped, the singers sang, and the trumpeters blew their trumpets. It was a joyous occasion indeed. All that were present with the king bowed themselves with Hezekiah and worshiped Jehovah. And this was only phase one of Hezekiah's great revival.

In phase two he sent word to all Israel and Judah that they should come to the house of the Lord at Jerusalem and keep the Passover. This is the first recorded ceremony of Passover-keeping since the time of Joshua, hundreds of years earlier. How low the people of God must have sunk during these turbulent years.

The heart of Jehovah must have been thrilled to see a man so concerned with the spiritual well-being of His people that he would restore the house of God, cleanse it, reinstitute the services and sacrifices in it, and rise early in the morning to worship Him. All of this was just the beginning of Hezekiah's reforms. How it would thrill the heart of Jehovah to see a man like Hezekiah raised up today to reform the worship of Israel once again. Let's pray to that end. Pray for the salvation of God's people and for the peace of Jerusalem.

MORNING HYMN

> *Revive Thy work, O Lord!*
> *Thy mighty arm make bare;*
> *Speak with the voice that wakes the dead,*
> *And make Thy people hear.*

God's Unfailing Word

MORNING SCRIPTURE   Luke 21:1-38
MORNING VERSE   Luke 21:38

And all the people came early in the morning to Him in the temple, for to hear Him.

THROUGHOUT His teaching ministry Jesus enjoyed an increasing appreciation for His message. Thousands thronged around Him, not only to view His powers of healing and raising the dead, but also to hear His words. Jesus was more than a prophet, a priest, and a king. The gospel writers describe Him as a preacher and a teacher as well. Just before the Passion Week Luke records that Jesus taught daily in the Temple, "And all the people came *early in the morning* to Him in the temple, for to hear Him" (Luke 21:38). His message was not just novel; it was truth.

Much of what Jesus taught daily in the Temple was prophetic in nature. In the early part of Luke 21 Jesus passed through the temple treasury and commented on the splendor of the magnificent Temple. However, Jesus predicted that it would be destroyed and His words are descriptive of the days leading up to the destruction of Jerusalem by the Romans in A.D. 70.

The latter half of this chapter is a prophecy concerning Jerusalem during the great tribulation period of this earth. He describes it as a time in which there shall be signs in the sun, the moon, and the stars. Men's hearts will fail them for fear. The powers of the heavens shall be shaken. Jesus taught the crowds who followed Him early in the morning to the Temple that God would unleash His vengeance on a sinful world before the Son of Man rode out of Heaven in power and great glory to establish His kingdom on this earth (cf. Revelation 19:11-16).

As the people came daily to hear the teachings of the Lord He knew that His time was quickly coming to an end on this earth. Therefore He reminded them that "Heaven and earth shall pass away: but My words shall not pass away" (Luke 21:33). It is evident that the Word of God, whether given verbally by the Lord Jesus or inscribed by God in the Holy Bible, is more unshakable than the universe itself. The same God who has the power to shake the very heavens also has the power to make unshakable

His Word. While the heavens will not stand according to the prophecy of Jesus, the Word of God will always stand.

Today, in the twentieth century, Jesus does not speak to us and teach us as He did early in the morning in the Temple, but He still speaks to us through His Word, God's Word—the Holy Bible. We have the benefit of hearing the very same teaching that these heard who came at the dawning of the day to the Temple. We can sit at the feet of Jesus today by reading His Word.

H. A. Ironside told of a godly man named Andrew Frazer who had come to southern California to recover from a serious illness. Though this Irishman was quite weak, he opened his worn Bible and began expounding the truths of God's Word in a way that Ironside had never heard before. So moved by Frazer's words was Ironside that his curiosity drove him to ask, "Where did you learn these things? Did you learn them in some college or seminary?" The sickly man said, "My dear young man, I learned these things on my knees on the mud floor of a little sod cottage in the north of Ireland. There with my open Bible before me I used to kneel for hours at a time and ask the Spirit of God to reveal Christ to my soul and to open the Word to my heart. He taught me more on my knees on that mud floor than I ever could have learned in all the seminaries or colleges in the world."

To spend time in the Word of God yields a much richer understanding of the deep things of theology than to spend time in a classroom. For the person denied a formal education in Bible and theology, there is no shame if we spend time at the feet of Jesus. From early in the morning, throughout the day, and into the evening hours the great scholars of the Word become so because of time spent in God's book and on their knees. Each of us has the same opportunity to do that. Let's take that opportunity today.

MORNING HYMN

> *Thy Word is like a garden, Lord,*
> *With flowers bright and fair;*
> *And ev'ryone who seeks may pluck*
> *A lovely cluster there.*
> *Thy Word is like a deep, deep mine,*
> *And jewels rich and rare*
> *Are hidden in its mighty depths*
> *For ev'ry searcher there.*

Effective Prayer

MORNING SCRIPTURE   2 Kings 19:1–37
MORNING VERSE   2 Kings 19:35

And it came to pass that night, that the angel of the LORD went out, and smote in the camp of the Assyrians an hundred fourscore and five thousand: and when they arose early in the morning, behold, they were all dead corpses.

KING HEZEKIAH was in a jam. Although he had trusted God, and did that which was right in the sight of the Lord, nonetheless his Assyrian enemy was knocking at his door. Sennacherib had sent three of his lieutenants to Jerusalem with a great host of Assyrian soldiers. Rab-shakeh, the spokesman for this terrible trio, taunted the Israelites, ridiculing their faith in Jehovah. He stood before the wall of Jerusalem shouting obscenities to the Jews and counseling them, "Let not Hezekiah deceive you . . . Neither let Hezekiah make you trust in the LORD . . . hearken not to Hezekiah. . . . Make an agreement with me" (2 Kings 18:29-31).

When the king heard that the Assyrians were outside the city walls, he rent his clothes, covered himself with sackcloth, and went into the house of the Lord. Here Isaiah the prophet encouraged Hezekiah that God had the situation well in control. Soon Hezekiah received a letter from the king of Assyria demanding that he surrender the city. What Hezekiah did next is characteristic of a man of faith. Hezekiah prayed unto the Lord God and in his prayer we can see the elements of all righteous prayer.

1. His prayer was *instinctively spontaneous* (verse 14). When Hezekiah received the threatening letter, he immediately spread it before the Lord. There was no thought of calling a committee or seeking the advice of others; Hezekiah knew what to do, as did Elisha (2 Kings 4:33) and Nehemiah (Nehemiah 2:4) in similar situations.

2. His prayer was *praisefully reverent* (verse 15). He addressed Jehovah as, "O LORD God of Israel, which dwellest between the cherubims, Thou art the God, even Thou alone." The Lord's Prayer (Matthew 6:9) indicates the same kind of reverence.

3. His prayer was *intimately personal* (verse 16). After he

addressed God in a reverent fashion, Hezekiah said, "LORD, bow down Thine ear and hear." He had recognized God as sovereign; now he addresses Him as friend.

4. His prayer was *respectfully informative* (verses 17-18). Hezekiah did not demand of God what should be done. He was reminding himself in prayer of what God had promised. When we inform God of our situation in prayer, it is not because He is unaware of how desperate we are; we do it so we are aware of how desperate we are.

5. His prayer was *purposefully direct* (verse 19a). The time had come to get down to business. He pointedly made his request known unto the Lord. "O LORD our God, I beseech thee, save Thou us out of his hand." Hezekiah did not mince words; he was direct and forthright in his request to God.

6. His prayer was *properly motivated* (verse 19b). Hezekiah prayed for deliverance from the Assyrians, "that all the kingdoms of the earth may know that thou art the LORD God, even Thou only." Anything that happens to God's people reflects on God's purpose. Our prayers ought to be motivated so that the world sees the grace of God in our deliverance from desperate situations.

7. His prayer was *powerfully effective* and 2 Kings 19:35-36 shows the powerful effect of the righteous man's prayer. "And it came to pass that night, that the angel of the LORD went out, and smote in the camp of the Assyrians an hundred fourscore and five thousand: and when they arose *early in the morning*, behold, they were all dead corpses." Early the next morning Hezekiah and the Jews found their enemy routed and 185,000 dead soldiers. God had performed what He promised.

Prayer is the power that gets ahold of God. Each of us would be wise to study carefully Hezekiah's prayer and see how these seven characteristics of his prayer can be applied to our prayer lives. Let's be like Hezekiah and believe that "the effectual fervent prayer of a righteous man availeth much" (James 5:16).

MORNING HYMN

> *I must tell Jesus all of my trials,*
> *I cannot bear these burdens alone;*
> *In my distress He kindly will help me,*
> *He ever loves and cares for His own.*

Our Majestic God

MORNING SCRIPTURE   Exodus 19:1-25
MORNING VERSE   Exodus 19:16

And it came to pass on the third day in the morning, that there were thunders and lightnings, and a thick cloud upon the mount, and the voice of the trumpet exceeding loud; so that all the people that was in the camp trembled.

T HE WANING YEARS of the twentieth century will undoubtedly be remembered both as an era of mushrooming technology and vanishing virtue. As the world's scientific achievements increase, its moral discernment declines. Institutions once sacred are now scorned. Beliefs that our less sophisticated forefathers revered and respected are now relinquished and ridiculed. The last third of this century has spawned a noticeable decrease in reverence and this tendency is nowhere more evident than in religion. Even the church has a grossly inadequate appreciation of who God is and how He should be revered.

In the third month after the exodus, Israel entered the desert of Sinai and encamped at the foot of the great mountain. As God's representative, Moses was summoned to Mount Sinai. Here God revealed that He would make Israel a "peculiar treasure" unto Himself above all other people. They would be a kingdom of priests and a holy nation if they would but obey God's voice and keep His covenant. Moses returned to the people with this proposition and they all agreed.

In three days the covenant would be established but the holiness of Almighty God is so awesome that much preparation would have to be made before the Israelites could enjoy His presence. Only the pure in heart can "see" God. Moses was to sanctify the people for two days. They were to wash their clothes, an outward sign of the fact that they were inwardly clean. This cleansing within must stem from a heartfelt repentance, deep contrition, and a sincere desire to live righteously before God. Such preparation each man had to make for himself. In addition, fences or barriers were to be set up in public preparation to meet God. To impress Israel with the awesome majesty of God and the reverence with which they should meet Him, the mountain was itself declared holy—off limits to everyone but Moses and Aaron. None could touch it or even approach it beyond the fences.

With the preparations made and the people standing by in silent awe, "It came to pass on the third day *in the morning*, that there were thunders and lightnings, and a thick cloud upon the mount, and the voice of the trumpet exceeding loud; so that all the people that was in the camp trembled" (Exodus 19:16). The reverence for God that this event was designed to instill in Israel renders vain any attempt to describe adequately the scene.

The Holy One of Israel appeared in a thick cloud because His presence was awesome, too tremendous to be seen physically. Accompanying the clapping of thunder was the voice of the trumpet, exceedingly loud. So terrifying was the trumpet that the people in the camp below were dumbfounded. They stood in mute reverence to the holiness of Almighty God. The whole mountain quaked greatly, shaking from top to bottom, as the people stood in amazement.

The awfulness and terror of this event is even more remarkable when we consider that God was not descending to Mount Sinai as Israel's Judge. He was not about to pronounce a sentence of doom on them but in love He was drawing them unto Himself through the Sinai covenant. The smoke, fire, cloud, trumpet, lightning, and thunder were all to bring Israel to revere Him for He is holy and almighty. He is of incredible majesty.

Although it is the duty of the Christian to praise God, it is our first duty to revere and fear Him. He alone is worthy of all reverence. "Wherefore receiving a kingdom which cannot be moved, let us have grace, by which we may serve God acceptably with reverence and godly fear; For our God is a consuming fire" (Hebrews 12:28-29). Let's revere the Lord today, and spend some time praising Him for who He is.

MORNING HYMN

> *Praise ye the Lord, the Almighty,*
> *The King of creation!*
> *O my soul, praise Him,*
> *For He is thy health and salvation!*
> *All ye who hear,*
> *Now to His temple draw near;*
> *Join me in glad adoration!*

Morning Mercies

MORNING SCRIPTURE   Lamentations 3:1-36
MORNING VERSE   Lamentations 3:22-23

It is of the LORD's mercies that we are not consumed, because His compassions fail not. They are new every morning; great is Thy faithfulness.

THE BOOK OF LAMENTATIONS may be the saddest writing in the ancient Near East. Composed of five chapters, each chapter is an elegy, almost a funeral dirge. Each of these elegies is sad beyond description. The whole of the book of Lamentations is a poem of pain, a symphony of sorrow. Lamentations has been called the wailing wall of the Bible, and so it is. The tears shed with each distressing chapter only increase as the Lamentations progress. There is but one bright spot in the five lamentations. This bright spot is our devotional for today.

In the midst of the most monstrous dirge of despair, the Prophet Jeremiah issues a remarkable testimony to the breadth and the force of divine grace. The black clouds which characterize the Lamentations are not universal; there is a minute break in those clouds through which the brightest sunlight streams forth. The penetrating rays of Lamentations 3:22-23 find their way through the chinks and crannies of the deepest dungeon. In the midst of his despondency over the destruction of Jerusalem, Jeremiah sees a ray of hope which depicts the unceasing mercies of God.

Although we have no claim on God's mercies, and they are altogether undeserved, nonetheless they never cease. We have done much to provoke God and give Him cause to cut off His mercy in our behalf. We have abused His mercy, ignored His mercy, even at times ungratefully accepted His mercy. Still, while God's mercies may not always be visible, they are always present. The mercies of God may change their form, as the morning light varies from the evening light, but the mercies of God will never cease to give their light. Even chastisement is mercy in disguise and frequently, under the circumstances which make chastisement necessary, it proves to be more merciful than had not God chastised us at all.

In the ray of sunlight presented by Lamentations 3:22-23, we learn that not only are the mercies of God not consumed, "They are new *every morning*," proving the great faithfulness of God.

There is great novelty in human life. Each day brings to us new and difficult problems, new and exciting challenges. God's mercy is ever-present with us, but the form it takes is ever-changing. God adapts His mercy to our immediate needs of each day. His mercies are not chiseled in stone but are vital and vibrant. We need not exhume the antique mercies which God showered on Moses, Jeremiah, or John. God's mercies on our behalf are fresh and alive today. As God renews His world by greening it every spring, so too He refreshes and invigorates His people by renewing His mercies to them every morning.

With every new morning, nature offers a tribute of praise to God's mercy. The sun rises, the birds sing, the trees sway in the breeze. Shall we alone be silent and ungrateful? Shall the Christian, who has the most reason to praise God for His mercy, be slow to acknowledge that God's mercy is renewed to him each day? Will we allow the natural creation of God alone to praise its Creator?

No matter how dark our day may appear to be, let us remember this with Jeremiah, "It is of the LORD'S mercies that we are not consumed, because His compassions fail not. They are new every morning; great is Thy faithfulness" (Lamentations 3:22-23).

MORNING HYMN

> *Great is Thy faithfulness, O God my Father!*
> *There is no shadow of turning with Thee;*
> *Thou changest not, Thy compassions, they fail not:*
> *As Thou hast been Thou forever wilt be.*
> *Great is Thy faithfulness! Great is Thy faithfulness!*
> *Morning by morning new mercies I see;*
> *All I have needed Thy hand hath provided—*
> *Great is Thy faithfulness, Lord, unto me!*

A Long Day

MORNING SCRIPTURE   Acts 28:1-31
MORNING VERSE   Acts 28:23

And when they had appointed him a day, there came many to him into his lodging; to whom he expounded and testified the kingdom of God, persuading them concerning Jesus, both out of the law of Moses, and out of the prophets, from morning till evening.

B IBLE STUDENTS find many parallels between what they read in the Word of God and what they see in the animal kingdom. Many of God's creatures have been singled out as examples of various kinds of activities. We are all familiar with the expression, "Busy as a bee." Although perhaps not as noticeable, the activity of others of God's creatures is just as great as that of the bee. For example, the thrush gets up at 2:30 every morning, begins work at once and does not stop until 9:30 at night. That's a whole nineteen-hour day. During that period of time this bird feeds its hungry fledglings about two hundred times. While the busyness of the bee is more noticeable, the activity of the thrush is equally as productive.

Astounding parallels can be drawn between the life of the Apostle Paul and the busy activity of the bees and the long days of the thrush. When Paul was saved on the road to Damascus, the Bible says, "Straightway he preached Christ in the synagogues, that He is the Son of God" (Acts 9:20). Paul may have said something like this to God at his salvation, "Lord, if you save me, the world will never hear the end of it!" It never did.

In this last chapter of Acts the apostle completes his tortuous journey to Rome and arrives to be placed under house arrest until his hearing before Caesar. It would have been a time for rest, recuperation from the rigors of the voyage, and restoration. No one would have criticized Paul for a lack of activity. He could have rationalized that to preach Christ in this situation only would have jeopardized his case before Caesar and perhaps ultimately cut short his ministry. Still, "There came many to him into his lodgings; to whom he expounded and testified the kingdom of God, persuading them concerning Jesus both out of the law of

Moses and out of the prophets, *from morning till evening"* (Acts 28:23).

He had just spent two years in prison at Caesarea. Since he was a Roman citizen, his final appeal was always to Caesar. While enroute to Rome a tempestuous wind arose, the ship was tossed to and fro for fourteen days and finally ran aground. With the others, Paul had to swim to shore, clinging to broken pieces of the ship. As if that were not enough, on shore he was bitten by a viper, but did not die. After three months they continued their journey, finally arriving at Rome. All this occurred just before Acts 28:23. From early in the morning until late at night he continued his preaching and teaching activity. No one asked him to put in such a long day, especially after the trials of the preceding months. Paul did it as a volunteer in the service of the Lord.

More importantly, the busyness of his activity was not in defense of his apostleship or in spinning yarns of his shipwreck. His activity was entirely a witness to the grace of God. He expounded and testified of the kingdom of God and persuaded them of the messiahship of Jesus. He had the right method; he preached unto them. He had the right message; he preached Jesus unto them. He had the right manner; he preached Jesus unto them from morning until evening.

Even toward the end of his recorded ministry, the Apostle Paul put in a long day of activity for the Lord. You and I have the same responsibility, the same opportunity, the same message as did the apostle. We must be as busy as a bee and put in a day like the thrush, with the message which stirred the heart of the apostle, if we are to rest at the end of this day fully satisfied of our service to the Lord God. Let's make sure we're satisfied tonight.

MORNING HYMN

Give of your best to the Master,
Give Him first place in your heart;
Give Him first place in your service,
Consecrate ev'ry part.

God's Abiding Presence

MORNING SCRIPTURE   1 Samuel 11:1-15
MORNING VERSE   1 Samuel 11:11

And it was so on the morrow, that Saul put the people in three companies; and they came into the midst of the host in the morning watch, and slew the Ammonites until the heat of the day: and it came to pass, that they which remained were scattered, so that two of them were not left together.

ONCE in scorn an unbeliever asked a Christian, "Where is God?" The Christian immediately responded, "Let me first ask you, 'Where is He not?'"

Saul had become Israel's first king but his leadership had not yet been tested. He did not have to wait long, however, until an opportunity arose for him to lead Israel decisively. During the latter years of Samuel's life the enemies of Israel had gained significant strength. One of those enemies was the Ammonites who dwelt east of the Jordan River. Nahash, the Ammonite, marched against the city of Jabesh-gilead, which was nestled in the thickly wooded hills east of the Sea of Galilee. This fertile farm district was of great importance to the Ammonites who generally lived in an arid land.

When Nahash laid seige to Jabesh-gilead he offered the inhabitants of the city an opportunity to make a covenant with him and to serve him as docile slaves. This probably would have been accepted had not Nahash made one unacceptable provision in this covenant. In utter contempt, he would only accept servitude from the Israelites if they would agree to allow him to put out the right eye of all the inhabitants of the city. In an unusual act of mercy, the Ammonites permitted the Israelites seven days to make their decision.

Immediately a Gileadite runner was dispatched to bring this distressing news to Israel's new king. Nahash's audacity fanned the spark of leadership in Saul and he immediately took a yoke of oxen and hewed them in pieces, sending one piece to each tribe throughout Israel and warning them that they would meet a similar fate if they did not rally behind Samuel and himself to fight against the Ammonites. Immediately three hundred thousand warriors of Israel and thirty thousand men of Judah assem-

bled at Bezek in order to march on Gilead and repel the Ammonite forces.

A message was sent ahead to the men of Jabesh-gilead
saying that tomorrow, by the time the sun was hot, they would
have help from the rest of Israel. *On the morrow* Saul moved into
the host of the Ammonites *in the morning watch* with three army
divisions and slew them until the heat of the day (1 Samuel
11:11). The victory over Ammon was complete. God acted swiftly
and early in the morning.

Perhaps Nahash the Ammonite attempted to enslave the
city of Jabesh-gilead because it was on the eastern side of the
Jordan River. Maybe he thought that the God of Israel resided
only in the promised land and would not be concerned with the
two and one-half tribes in the hinterland. But God's people have
His promise that He is always close at hand. "Do not I fill heaven
and earth saith the LORD?" (Jeremiah 23:24). God's abiding presence is ever with His people and Satan and his henchmen must
never feel free to lay seige to the people of God just because they
are living on the fringe of God's activity.

A nineteenth century Scottish churchman named Chalmers
once wrote, "When I walk by the wayside, He is along with me,
when I enter into company amid all my forgetfulness of Him, He
never forgets me. In the silent watches of the night, when my
eyelids are closed and my spirit has sunk into unconsciousness,
the observant eye of Him who never slumbers is upon me. I
cannot flee from His presence. Go where I will, He leads me, and
watches me, and cares for me."

If you are one of God's children, you need never feel forsak-
en, abandoned, or alone. You need never worry about the attacks
of men like Nahash simply because you dwell where there is
lessened opportunity for service to the Lord or in years when
bustling activity for the Lord has passed you by. God is as much
interested in the two and one-half tribes of Israel east of the
Jordan as He is in the tribes dwelling in the promised land. You
have the promise of His abiding presence just as much as others
do. Claim that promise throughout this day.

MORNING HYMN

> *Anywhere with Jesus I am not alone;*
> *Other friends may fail me, He is still my own;*
> *Tho' His hand may lead me over dreary ways,*
> *Anywhere with Jesus is a house of praise.*

Yielding to God

MORNING SCRIPTURE   *Genesis 32:1-32*
MORNING VERSE   *Genesis 32:24*

*And Jacob was left alone; and there wrestled a man with him
until the breaking of the day.*

JACOB was in big trouble. He was caught between his two
greatest enemies. Behind him was his avaricious father-in-law,
Laban. Before him was his vindictive brother, Esau. The patriarch wasn't exactly on speaking terms with either of these men.
He had secretly left Laban's household in order to return to the
promised land. Would Laban now honor the covenant they had
made at Mizpah (Genesis 31:49)? Jacob wasn't sure. But even if
Jacob had nothing to fear from Laban, there was still Esau.

Earlier in his life Jacob had craftily deprived his twin brother of both his birthright and his father's blessing. Now for the first
time in twenty years he was about to encounter the brother
whom he had wronged. Esau had become a powerful man in
Mount Seir, the land of Edom. How would he react to the news
that his supplanting brother had returned? Jacob sent messengers
to break the news to Esau gently but these men returned with the
distressing report that Esau was coming to meet his brother with
four hundred armed men.

As his apprehension increased, Jacob sought the Lord in
earnest prayer. Confessing that he was unworthy of the least of
the Lord's mercies, Jacob asked for deliverance from the hand of
his brother. After a season of prevailing prayer, Jacob sent gifts of
his flocks and herds to Esau in hope of appeasing his brother's
wrath. Then he rose up at night and sent away his wives and
eleven sons for safety.

This left Jacob alone on the north bank of the brook Jabbok.
It was dark, perhaps shortly after midnight. As Jacob returned to
prayer, suddenly a man appeared in the inky darkness and attacked him. Jacob's first reaction must have been that this attacker
was his brother Esau seeking revenge. Back and forth they wrestled and at first it seemed to be an even match. The wrestlers
appeared to be equal in strength and skill so that neither emerged
victorious. The fight dragged on all night. Then, at *the breaking o*

the day, the stranger touched the hollow of Jacob's thigh and it was thrown out of joint (Gen. 32:24-25). Suddenly Jacob realized that his antagonist was no ordinary man but the Angel Jehovah and that it was only God's grace and not Jacob's ability that the wrestling match had lasted as long as it did.

Over the years the Lord had been striving with Jacob. Yet the patriarch persisted in charting his own course, scheming, "wheeling and dealing" in order to be blessed. He was a man of a divided mind; he wanted to trust God and commit his life to Him but he wanted to rely on human devices as well. Jacob was miserable for he had not yet learned that an unsatisfied life results from an unsurrendered will.

When the light of day broke the wrestling match ended. Before Jacob would let the Lord go, however, he sought a reconfirmation of the blessing given him years before at Bethel. With Esau approaching it was important for Jacob to know that he was the heir of God. At this point the heavenly wrestler said, "Thy name shall be called no more Jacob, but Israel; for as a prince hast thou power with God and with men, and hast prevailed." Jacob had physically lost the wrestling match but had spiritually gained the victory. He had been emptied of his self-will, drained of his last effort to win in his own strength. Yet emptiness is the cup into which God pours blessing.

As the sun rose upon him, Jacob passed over Penuel, where he had seen God face to face, and discovered that he limped on his thigh. For the rest of his life he bore this physical reminder of that fateful wrestling match with the Lord.

When in prayer the Lord wrestles our will from us we may also bear some mark for the rest of our lives, but it will be worth it. One day in which our will is yielded to Him is worth a hundred years of striving to please Him in our own strength. "For it is God who worketh in you both to will and to do of His good pleasure" (Philippians 2:13).

MORNING HYMN

> *O Love that wilt not let me go,*
> *I rest my weary soul on Thee;*
> *I give Thee back the life I owe,*
> *That in Thine ocean depths its flow*
> *May richer, fuller be.*

Perfect Promises

MORNING SCRIPTURE   *Joshua 6:1-27*
MORNING VERSE   *Joshua 6:15*

And it came to pass on the seventh day, that they rose early about the dawning of the day, and compassed the city after the same manner seven times: only on that day they compassed the city seven times.

EVERY few years the countries of the free world participate in national elections. The democratic system of government provides the opportunity for men and women representing their parties to campaign, make promises and pledges, and run for office on the basis of their platform and promises. Generally the winner is the person who promises the most and who, in the minds of the voters, can actually deliver on those campaign promises. Unfortunately history has taught us that most political promises are little more than campaign rhetoric and the voters have justifiable reason for concern about their validity. In contrast to this are the promises of God in which the believer may have absolute confidence. God has a perfect record of keeping His promises.

The story of Jericho's conquest is a fine example of the completed promises of God. Prior to their entrance into the promised land, Joshua sent two men across the Jordan to spy out the city of Jericho. These spies came to the place where information would freely flow among the men of the town. They entered the house of Rahab the harlot. Although the life of Rahab as a harlot was certainly not condoned by the Israeli spies, nevertheless apparently the Lord God had been working in the heart of Rahab. When the king of Jericho attempted to track down the two spies, Rahab hid them on her roof among the sticks of flax. She confessed her faith in Jehovah God saying, "The LORD your God, he is God in heaven above, and in earth beneath" (Joshua 2:11). Because this woman aided His secret agents, God promised Rahab and her household salvation in the midst of the peril of her city.

God's battle plan for the defeat of Jericho was unconventional, to say the least. Joshua would command seven priests bearing seven trumpets of ram's horns before the ark of the Lord to march around the city walls in silence for seven days, once each day until the seventh. On the seventh day they would march seven times around the wall. Then amid the blast of the seven jubilee trumpets and the war cry of the people of God, the destruction of the stronghold at Jericho would take place.

The children of Israel did as God commanded. "And it came to pass on the seventh day, that *they rose early about the dawning of the day* and compassed the city after the same manner seven times" (Joshua 6:15). On the seventh circuit of the seventh day the people shouted and the walls of Jericho fell down flat. The army of Israel entered the city unhindered and utterly destroyed all that was in the city, with one notable exception—the household of Rahab. Because they obeyed the Lord explicitly, the people saw two great promises of the Lord performed on the same day. The city of Jericho, the strongest outpost of the Canaanite defenses, had been utterly destroyed as God had promised. Likewise Rahab and her household had been spared destruction, as God had promised.

But there is one final promise of God that can be seen in the conquest of Jericho. In verse 26 Joshua counseled the people, warning them, "Cursed be the man before the LORD, that riseth up and buildeth this city Jericho: he shall lay the foundation thereof in his firstborn, and in his youngest son shall he set up the gates of it." To show that God means business when He makes a promise, Joshua imprecated a solemn curse on anyone who would rebuild the now-destroyed Jericho. This curse was literally fulfilled in the fate of Heil, the Bethelite, who rebuilt Jericho in the reign of Ahab (about 925 B.C.). Heil's firstborn son, Abiram, died as he was laying the foundation for the rebuilding of Jericho. Also his youngest son, Segub, died while he was setting up the gates of the city (1 Kings 16:34). What God promises, God performs.

Whether the promise is for salvation, as in the case of Rahab, or for destruction, as in the case of Heil, the promises of God must never be taken lightly. Whatever God promises, God performs. You can count on it.

MORNING HYMN

> *Standing on the promises that cannot fail,*
> *When the howling storms of doubt and fear assail,*
> *By the living word of God I shall prevail,*
> *Standing on the promises of God.*

Friendship

MORNING SCRIPTURE   2 Samuel 16:15–17:24
MORNING VERSE   2 Samuel 17:22

Then David arose, and all the people that were with him, and they passed over Jordan: by the morning light there lacked not one of them that was not gone over Jordan.

O NE of the prize gems of human relationships is friendship. Emerson said, "The only way to have a friend is to be one," an echo of Proverbs 18:24. Friendship always enriches our lives, but sometimes it preserves them as well. The friendship of Hushai with David is a fine example.

Nathan's prophecy upon David for his great sin was severe and swift in coming. It struck first with David's son Amnon, and quickly thereafter with the hot-tempered Absalom. Absalom's rebellion against his father had taken firm root in Israel. He was clearly in command and was now residing in Jerusalem. But the aura of David's presence in Israel and the legend of his prowess as a man of war made Absalom's rebellion tenuous. He must pursue his own father and the warriors who were with him. How would this be done?

Absalom's close advisor, Ahithophel, hatched a plan, the sagacity of which was unrivaled. He proposed that the armies of Israel pursue David with twelve thousand chosen men and fall on him when David and his soldiers were weary and sapped of strength. They would kill David only. What is most unbelievable is that Absalom readily agreed that this was a good plan. But in the providence of God, Absalom opted to get another opinion before he enacted it. Thus he called Hushai the Archite. Although pretending allegiance to Absalom, Hushai remained the loyal friend of David and acted as his informer revealing Absalom's every move.

The plan of Hushai was a classic case of overkill. He called for Absalom to gather Israel from Dan to Beersheba, as many as the sand of the sea, against David in battle. His rhetoric must have appeared venomous and thus Absalom liked the plan even more than that of Ahithophel. The foolish Absalom did not know that this plan was divinely originated and calculated for his own destruction. "For the Lord had appointed to defeat the good counsel of Ahithophel, to the intent that the Lord might bring evil upon Absalom."

No sooner was the plan accepted by Absalom than Hushai dispatched Zadok and Abiathar the priests to warn David of the impending danger. David arose and all his men passed over the Jordan River *by the morning light* (2 Samuel 17:22). They were taking no chances; they fled at the rising of the sun. It is always a wise decision to flee evil at the beginning of the day.

Absalom pursued his father across the Jordan River and the famous incident of catching his long-flowing hair in the boughs of a great oak tree occurred that day. That day Absalom was killed. God had crushed an evil rebellion against His ordained king through the loyalty and godly commitment of a friend.

Visitors to the Ft. Myers, Florida, home of Thomas Alva Edison, are intrigued by a path in his garden which he called "the walk of friendship." The uniqueness of this walk is that each of the stones which constitute the walk was given to Edison by a friend. The pathway is designed as a memorial to friendship, the kind of friend that Hushai was to David, for friends lead friends step by step out of danger into delight.

If you have a close friend, rejoice in that friend and thank God for him or her. Enjoy that bond of friendship which you have. In fact, why not write or call that friend today and tell him you love him in the Lord and are praying for him. You'll never know what it will mean to him if you don't.

MORNING HYMN

> *What a Friend we have in Jesus,*
> *All our sins and griefs to bear!*
> *What a privilege to carry*
> *Ev'rything to God in prayer!*
> *O what peace we often forfeit,*
> *O what needless pain we bear,*
> *All because we do not carry*
> *Ev'ry thing to God in prayer.*

Awake Early

MORNING SCRIPTURE   Psalm 108:1-13
MORNING VERSE   Psalm 108:2

Awake, psaltery and harp: I myself will awake early.

A RE YOU a morning person? Do you know others who claim to be night people? If so, whether morning person or night person, each of us must ask ourselves if our heart is fixed upon God.

David wrote in Psalm 108, "O God, my heart is fixed; I will sing and give praise, even with my glory." Whether a morning person or a night person, the one who knows and loves the Lord God can have an unperturbed heart when he sees the world reeling around him. Our hearts bow to sing and give praise with all our intellect, our skills, our resources, ourselves. It is the call to obey the command of the unperturbed heart which causes us to rise in the morning with a song on our lips. David, an early riser, not only resolved to sing and give praises to God with his lips, but resolved to employ the use of musical instruments in that same melody of praise. He implores, "Awake, psaltery and harp." Not content with singing the praises of God alone, he will use the well-tuned strings of the psaltery and harp and his flying fingers to accompany his vocal chords.

Still, the key to his praise for God is not found in his voice or in the psaltery and harp. The key is found in his call to "awake" himself to the lively pursuit of praise to God. It is only when a thoroughly enraptured soul sings to God that his vocal praise is acceptable to Him. David says, "Awake, psaltery and harp: I myself will awake *early*" (Psalm 108:2). His praise to the Lord God will precede the dawn. The best and brightest hours of the day will find the psalmist heartily aroused to bless God. Not only will he awaken early to praise Him but he will awaken every fiber of his being to praise God. Some engage in praise to God in a halfhearted manner; these sing in drawling tones, as if they were half asleep. They arise early to praise God but do not awaken their minds, their spirits, and their bodies in praise to God. Early risers who seek to please the Lord must make certain that they have awakened themselves thoroughly before they begin to praise

Him or their practice of predawn praise will be reduced to mere ritualism.

Having a time alone with God early in the morning is a blessed experience. But too often our prayer life early in the morning is burdened down with weariness, sleepiness, and a half-awake attitude toward God. When we have our morning devotions we must be certain that we are wide awake and ready to meet with God. Then will our meeting with the Almighty be something enjoyable, something vibrant, alive, and awake.

Henry Ward Beecher relates an incident about a laborer on his father's farm in Litchfield, Connecticut. Of this laborer he said: "He had a little room, in one corner of which I had a small cot, and as a boy I used to lie there and wonder at the enthusiasm with which he engaged in his devotions. It was a regular thing. First he would read the New Testament, hardly aware that I was in the room. Then he would alternately pray and sing and laugh. I never saw the Bible enjoyed like that! But I want to bear record that his praying made a profound impression upon me. It never entered my mind whether or not his actions were appropriate. I only thought, 'How that man does enjoy it!' I gained from him more of an idea of the desirableness of rejoicing prayer than I ever did from my mother or father. He led me to see that there should be real overflowing gladness and thanksgiving in it all."

Is it any wonder that when David's heart was fixed upon God he called himself to awaken early in praise of God. To have our minds ready, the psaltery and harp ready, but not ourselves ready is an affront to our early morning praise to God.

Let us always be alert, awake, and available to praise God early in the morning. Only as we are sufficiently alive to engage in a meaningful and enjoyable prayer life with God will He hear us when we pray, "Be thou exalted, O God, above the heavens, and Thy glory above all the earth."

MORNING HYMN

Oh, the pure delight of a single hour
That before Thy throne I spend,
When I kneel in prayer, and with Thee, my God,
I commune as friend with friend!

Fleece or Faith

MORNING SCRIPTURE   *Judges 6:16-40*
MORNING VERSE   *Judges 6:38*

And it was so: for he rose up early on the morrow, and thrust the fleece together, and wringed the dew out of the fleece, a bowl full of water.

DISCOURAGED AND PATHETIC Israel needed a champion. God had chosen His man. The angel of the Lord appeared unto Gideon, a mighty man of valor, and encouraged him with the promise of God's presence and power. Gideon had broken down the altar to Baal. Idolatry throughout the land of Israel was pounded with a heavy blow. Jehovah alone was now worshiped in Ophrah and the fame of Gideon spread throughout the land. It was apparent that Gideon was the man behind whom all Israel could rally.

Once again the Midianite Bedouins swarmed across the land. Gideon knew that the time for battle had come, but this time he was ready. Judges 6:34 says, "The Spirit of the LORD came upon Gideon," literally, the Spirit of Jehovah clothed Gideon like a garment. The once discouraged and despondent young farmer of Ophrah was now suited up for battle in the armor of the Spirit of God. When he sounded the mustering trumpet, immediately all of the clan of Abiezer gathered around him. Messengers were sent throughout all the land. From Naphtali, Zebulun, Asher, and Manasseh they came, prepared to fight under the leadership of Gideon.

All was ready for the mighty battle, yet one thing more troubled Gideon. Again he asked a sign from the Lord. Seeking a sign from God was characteristic of Jewish behavior (1 Corinthians 1:22). With troops arrayed for battle, Gideon spread a fleece of wool on the ground and said to the Lord God, "If the dew be on the fleece only, and it be dry upon all the earth beside, then shall I know that Thou wilt save Israel by mine hand, as Thou hast said." A heavy dew is very common in the highlands of Palestine. Even today clothes left outdoors overnight must be wrung out in the morning. Although energized for battle, the entire camp of Israel waited throughout the night for the sign from God.

The Scripture records that Gideon *rose up early on the morrow*, and wrung enough dew out of the fleece to fill a bowl full of water (Judges 6:38). Miracle accomplished! However, Gideon entreated the grace and patience of the Lord again and asked Jehovah to reverse the sign. One more night the Israelites waited before entering battle. In the morning the ground was saturated with dew but the fleece was entirely dry. This was proof positive that God was in this battle and that Gideon was His chosen leader.

Frequently much indecision and lack of courage is camouflaged under the guise of "putting out the fleece." Such a practice is not always an admirable one, nor does it always produce admirable results. When John Wesley was a thirty-two-year-old missionary in Georgia he fell deeply in love with a young woman he wanted to marry. Some of his friends suggested that perhaps God would have the evangelist remain unmarried and devote his life to his work. One even suggested they draw lots in order to discern God's will for Wesley. The evangelist agreed. Three small slips of paper were prepared: one said, "Marry"; the second, "Think not of it this year"; and the third, "Think of it no more." Wesley drew a slip and with much sadness read, "Think of it no more." Heartbroken, he ended his courtship. Fifteen years later Wesley married a wealthy widow who became a hindrance to his ministry. After twenty years of mutual misery, she left him. He had allowed a fleece to determine his fortune.

When God sets up the parameters, encourages us in a given situation, and calls us to action, let's not be guilty of "fleecing" Him. How much better if Gideon had been remembered for his faith, as was Abraham, than for his fleece. For what will you be remembered?

MORNING HYMN

> *I am trusting Thee, Lord Jesus,*
> *Trusting only Thee;*
> *Trusting Thee for full salvation,*
> *Great and free.*
> *I am trusting Thee to guide me,*
> *Thou alone shalt lead,*
> *Ev'ry day and hour supplying*
> *All my need.*

Incomplete Obedience

MORNING SCRIPTURE   1 Samuel 15:1-35
MORNING VERSE   1 Samuel 15:12

And when Samuel rose early to meet Saul in the morning, it was told Samuel, saying, Saul came to Carmel, and, behold, he set him up a place, and is gone about, and passed on, and gone down to Gilgal.

I NCOMPLETE OBEDIENCE is the half brother of disobedience. Not to obey God explicitly is to disobey Him implicitly. Saul is an example of this kind of disobedience.

Several great military victories over Moab, Ammon, Edom, and the kings of Zobah all strengthened Saul's position as king of Israel and secured for him the loyalty of the people. He was their hero, and he was beginning to know it.

Still, the great Bedouin tribe of the Amalekites continued to harass the Jews. In the past, at Sinai, in the wilderness, and in the days of Gideon, these Amalekites repeatedly attacked the Israelites without provocation. Thus, through the prophets, God told Saul to kill the wicked Amalekites and destroy all their livestock. He wanted His people to realize just how much He hates sin and thus God would not allow them to be enriched in any way by the conquests of their ungodly neighbors.

Mustering a force of two thousand infantrymen and an additional ten thousand men from Judah, Saul marched to the south against the Amalekites. Saul's victory over the Amalekites was complete and decisive. The Israelite army annihilated the entire tribe as God had commanded. But Saul did something that God did not command, in fact, something He explicitly prohibited. "And he took Agag the king of the Amalekites alive . . . and the people spared Agag and the best of the sheep and of the oxen, and of the fatlings, and the lambs, and all that was good, and would not utterly destroy them."

Twice before Saul had shown himself unfit for leadership because of his disobedience to God. Now God indicated to Samuel that Saul could no longer be king because of his disobedience and rebellion; he would be rejected by God. So distressing was this news to Samuel that he cried unto the Lord all night long, but to no avail. Jehovah's mind was set; Saul must go. Reluctant to deliver such a message to the king, and having wrestled about it with God all night, Samuel *rose early* to meet Saul *in the morning* (I Samuel 15:12).

When Samuel approached Saul at Gilgal, Saul piously greeted him, "Blessed be thou of the LORD," as if he had done nothing wrong. In fact he reported, "I have performed the commandment of the LORD." But Samuel knew otherwise and pointedly asked the king, "What meaneth then this bleating of the sheep in mine ears, and the lowing of the oxen which I hear?" Bleating sheep and lowing oxen are seldom informers, but in this instance they revealed the partial disbodience of the king, demonstrating again the principle of Numbers 32:23, "Be sure your sin will find you out."

Embarrassed that his disobedience had been discovered, but always ready with an explanation, Saul violated his leadership and squarely blamed the people for this sin. Samuel rehearsed in Saul's ears what the Lord had commanded him to do and how he had failed to keep the Lord's command. Assuming that the prophet would be pacified by the prospects of a sacrifice to Jehovah, Saul thought he had devised the perfect excuse for disobedience. How could God not be pleased with a sacrifice? But Samuel countered, "Hath the LORD as great delight in burnt offerings and sacrifices, as in obeying the voice of the LORD?" There was no answer. Saul was trapped in his disobedience.

The lesson that Saul failed to learn is one that we must not fail to learn from him. Samuel taught the king, "Behold, to obey is better than sacrifice." Obeying the voice of God can never become subservient to acts of worship or service. Obedience is the primary response necessary from a servant to his master. Partial obedience merely betrays rebellion against our master and thus pàrtial obedience is in reality disobedience. First, last, and always obedience is the very best thing.

MORNING HYMN

> *When we walk with the Lord*
> *In the light of His Word,*
> *What a glory He sheds on our way!*
> *While we do His good will*
> *He abides with us still,*
> *And with all who will trust and obey.*

Prayer and Peace

MORNING SCRIPTURE   Isaiah 26:1-21
MORNING VERSE   Isaiah 26:9

With my soul have I desired Thee in the night; yea, with my spirit within me will I seek Thee early: for when Thy judgments are in the earth, the inhabitants of the world will learn righteousness.

ONE OF THE PREVAILING THEMES of both Old and New Testaments is the constant presence of peace in the hearts of those who abide in God. The prophet Isaiah said it this way, "Thou wilt keep him in perfect peace, whose mind is stayed on Thee: because he trusteth in Thee" (Isaiah 26:3). Literally Isaiah said, "Thou wilt keep him in peace, peace" or, God will keep us in double peace, He will give us a double portion of peace when our minds rest on Him.

Likewise in the New Testament Jesus taught His disciples that His very presence would bring them peace. He said, "Peace I leave with you, My peace I give unto you: not as the world giveth give I unto you" (John 14:27). He told His disciples, "These things I have spoken unto you, that in Me ye might have peace. In the world ye shall have tribulation: but be of good cheer; I have overcome the world" (John 16:33).

The Apostle Paul understood the principle of fixing our minds on God and enjoying His peace. He counseled the Colossian believers to "let the peace of God rule in your hearts, to the which also ye are called in one body; and be ye thankful" (Colossians 3:15). If our minds are stayed upon God, His peace will rule the affairs entertained by our minds. If, on the other hand, we allow our minds to dwell on the cares of this world, God's peace will be far from our thoughts.

It is for this very reason that the apostle told the Philippian believers, "Be careful for nothing," or, be full of care about nothing, "but in everything by prayer and supplication with thanksgiving let your requests be made known unto God. And the peace of God, which passeth all understanding, shall keep your hearts and minds through Christ Jesus" (Philippians 4:6–7). The peace of God which garrisons our hearts and minds cannot exist alongside of the cares of this life. Each of us must make the decision whether our minds will dwell on those things that trouble us or on the power of God to deliver us. A mind full of care can be a mind full of peace. The difference is only a prayer away.

Isaiah was in the habit of seeking God in the middle of the night. When the thick clouds of sorrow overshadowed his heart and he no longer could endure the disappointments of that day, he did not allow his mind to dwell on those disappointments but rather on the Lord's deliverance. Rather than lay his head on a pillow of doubt, he would lay it on the pillow of dependence on the Lord God.

Isaiah continued, "Yea, with my spirit within me *will I seek Thee early*" (Isaiah 26:9). The experience of meeting the Lord in the darkness of midnight and having his mind freed from fear enabled the prophet to face the new day eagerly awaiting an additional measure of God's peace. Thus he determined that his spirit would seek the Lord early, fully confident that the Lord would answer his prayer: "Lord, Thou wilt ordain peace for us: for Thou also hast wrought all our works in us" (Isaiah 26:12).

The pattern for dealing with the cares of this world is the same for us today. God has designed us to live at peace with Him, with our world, and with ourselves. But we can do this only as we turn our cares over to Him in exchange for His ruling peace. Whatever difficulties you faced yesterday and wrestled with through the night last night, give them early this morning to the Lord and let Him replace your cares with the comfort of His peace. Remember, God's peace is but a prayer away.

MORNING HYMN

> *Peace! peace! wonderful peace,*
> *Coming down from the Father above;*
> *Sweep over my spirit forever, I pray,*
> *In fathomless billows of love.*

Reasonable Service

MORNING SCRIPTURE   *Exodus 24:1-18*
MORNING VERSE   *Exodus 24:4*

And Moses wrote all the words of the LORD, and rose up early in the morning, and builded an altar under the hill, and twelve pillars, according to the twelve tribes of Israel.

CONSECRATION to the Lord requires separation from evil, devotion to God, and the endless pursuit of holiness. Although the Lord would have all His children be fully consecrated to His service, He requires of us "reasonable" service (Romans 12:1). Consecration made under the influence of emotion or the excitement of the moment is not to be trusted. The believer must carefully, prayerfully, and reasonably count the cost of discipleship before committing his life in service to the Lord.

After the great law was given to Moses on Mount Sinai, God sought ratification of the covenant He had made with the Israelites. Once again Moses ascended the holy mountain, this time with Aaron, Nadab, Abihu, and seventy of the elders of Israel. When they descended again, Moses relayed to the people all the ordinances of God's covenant. As soon as the terms of the covenant were known, "the people answered with one voice, and said, All the words which the LORD hath said will we do" (Exodus 24:3). Immediately Moses sensed that the people were too readily consecrating themselves to the ordinances of God's covenant and had not counted the cost. Thus Moses maneuvered to make their consecration more reasonable.

First Moses purposefully prolonged the process of consecration. He did not permit the people to ratify the covenant at once. Instead, this great man of God wrote down all the words of the Lord and went to bed. He *"rose up early in the morning,* and builded an altar under the hill, and twelve pillars, according to the twelve tribes of Israel"* (Exodus 24:4). The altar was built in preparation for the sacrifice without which no covenant was considered binding. By making the people wait one day before they could officially ratify the covenant, Moses reduced the emotional influence of the Israelites' hasty acceptance of the covenant.

Secondly, Moses surrounded the ratification of the covenant

and the consecration with impressive ceremonies. He sent the young men, perhaps the firstborn of the families since the Levitical order had not yet been instituted, and they offered burnt offerings and sacrificed peace offerings of oxen unto the Lord. This was to be a solemn occasion, one which the Israelites would not soon forget.

Thirdly, great pains were taken to insure that the people understood the terms of the covenant. They could not properly consecrate themselves to God if they did not fully comprehend what their consecration meant. Not only did Moses relay the words of the Lord to the people when he descended from the mountain, but now, a day later, he read from the book of the covenant in the hearing of all the people. Moses wanted to be absolutely convinced that the people were making a rational decision to give their lives in service to the Lord.

Finally, Moses took the blood of the sacrifice and sprinkled it on the people saying, "Behold the blood of the covenant, which the LORD hath made with you concerning all these words." It was the blood which sealed the covenant. It was the symbol of the covenant. The blood of the sacrifice was placed upon the people to etch in their minds that they were chosen of God and now consecrated to Him.

Choosing a life of consecration to the Lord should be a sensible, reasonable, thoughtful act. The decision to give yourself to God and His service is a solemn act based in reason, not in emotion. It is indeed praiseworthy for a believer to consecrate his life to the Lord, but he must never do so lightly or thoughtlessly. Before committing your life in service to God today, count the cost, for "No man, having put his hand to the plough, and looking back, is fit for the kingdom of God" (Luke 9:62).

MORNING HYMN

> *All for Jesus, all for Jesus!*
> *All my being's ransomed pow'rs:*
> *All my tho'ts and words and doings,*
> *All my days and all my hours.*

The Gift of Criticism

MORNING SCRIPTURE   John 8:1–32
MORNING VERSE   John 8:2

And early in the morning He came again into the temple, and all the people came unto Him; and He sat down, and taught them.

I T WAS after a church service one morning in which the minister had preached on spiritual gifts that he was greeted at the door by a lady who said, "Pastor, I believe I have the gift of criticism." The pastor looked at her and asked, "Remember the person in Jesus' parable who had the one talent?" The woman nodded her understanding. "Do you recall what he did with it?" "Yes," replied the lady, "he went out and buried it." The pastor suggested, "Go, thou, and do likewise!"

The Pharisees and Sadducees apparently felt they too had the gift of criticism. Frequently they attempted to ensnare the Lord Jesus. As was the Master's habit, He entered Jerusalem crossing the Mount of Olives and *early in the morning* He came again into the temple, and all the people came unto Him; and He sat down and taught them" (John 8:2). His reappearance in the Temple provided an opportunity for the Pharisees and scribes to lay a subtle snare for Him. They brought a woman taken in the very act of adultery. The Feast of Tabernacles had just been celebrated and acts of immorality during that festive week were not unusual. The scribes attempted to put Christ in a dilemma by quoting the law of Moses. They knew that if He answered that the woman should be stoned, He would violate the Roman law which forbade such acts. However, if Jesus answered that the woman should not be stoned, He would be violating Moses' law (Deuteronomy 22:24).

The religious leaders were not so much interested in the adulterous woman as they were in Jesus' response to her situation. Their criticism of her was motivated by their desire to entrap Him. But Christ knew well how to repel such attacks by an appeal to higher principles. The same law which adjudged the guilty to be stoned to death also required the witnesses to cast the first stones. Jesus' statement, "He that is without sin among you, let him first cast a stone at her," was sure to bring an end to their criticism. The crowd, one by one, stealthily left the scene. Ironically enough, the only one who was left was the Lord Jesus, the only one of the crowd who had lived a perfect life and had a right to condemn her.

This very teaching is reiterated by the Apostle Paul in Romans 8. Paul asks the hypothetical questions, "What shall we then say to these things? If God be for us, who can be against us? . . . who shall lay anything to the charge of God's elect? It is God that justifieth. Who is he that condemneth? It is Christ that died, yea rather, that is risen again, who is even at the right hand of God, who also maketh intercession for us" (Romans 8:31, 33–34). Only the mind of God could conceive of a plan whereby the one person who lived a righteous life and had the right to condemn us was the very person who laid down that life to die for us. The woman taken in adultery was speaking to the one who did not come into the world to condemn the world, but to save the world.

One businessman keeps a fairly large stone on his desk. The stone is mounted and lettered with one word, "First." This acts as a constant reminder to him of Jesus' words, "He that is without sin . . . let him first cast a stone." When his employees enter his office and there is reason to criticize them for their lack of achievement, the man looks at the stone and recalls his own shortcomings. He deals with his employees in mercy and grace.

This passage of Scripture does not teach us to look the other way when people sin. It does not teach us that we ought to condone adultery or any other crime. What it does teach us, however, is that it is not the responsibility of a Christian continually to be on the lookout for sin in other Christians, or anyone else for that matter. If we have lived a perfect life, we can be a watchdog on others who have not lived a perfect life. But we have enough trouble keeping ourselves in line; we need not constantly be critical of the way others live. Jesus was teaching the critical religious leaders of His day that, although the woman was a great sinner, she was no greater a sinner than they were. We must remember the same as we meet others today.

MORNING HYMN

> *More like the Master I would live and grow,*
> *More of His love to others I would show;*
> *More self-denial, like His in Galilee,*
> *More like the Master I long to ever be.*

Glory to God

MORNING SCRIPTURE *Judges 7:1-25*
MORNING VERSE *Judges 7:1*

Then Jerubbaal, who is Gideon, and all the people that were with him, rose up early, and pitched beside the well of Harod: so that the host of the Midianites were on the north side of them, by the hill of Moreh, in the valley.

N ATURAL MAN has a penchant for trying to explain away God. The theory of evolution was developed in an attempt to remove God from the arena of creation. Liberal theologians have attempted to demythologize the Bible in order to remove the miraculous works of God from it. Man does all he can to explain naturally the divinely originated phenomena in our world.

God has always been aware of man's desire to usurp His position and authority. Frequently in Scripture can be found accounts where God places men in deliberate situations so they must recognize their deliverance is solely of Him. When God removes the possibility of any natural explanation, man is left with the inevitable conclusion that God is in the miracle business. Such was the case in our Scripture today.

Israel was assembled and ready for battle. Already the fight had been stayed two days by the dewy and dry fleece so that Gideon could receive a token of God's presence with them. Now the fight was to be delayed again.

On the morning following the second test with the fleece, Gideon and all the people with him "*rose up early* and pitched beside the well of Harod" (Judges 7:1). Anxious for the battle, they had already moved into military position when God told Gideon he had too many people in His army. Jehovah wanted to be certain that Gideon, as well as Israel and the nations watching, would understand that Israel had won the battle by the hand of God. Therefore he instructed Gideon to command any of the thirty-two thousand troops who were afraid to return home from the front. Much to the surprise of Gideon, twenty-two thousand admitted their fear and retreated. Surely if a battle were won by ten thousand Israeli troops against one hundred thirty-five thousand Midianites (Judges 8:10) this would indicate that the victory was the Lord's. But again Jehovah surprised Gideon by indicating that these ten thousand troops were still far too many.

Gideon was to take the troops to the spring of Harod for a strange and severe test. The soldiers were divided into two groups, those who lapped water as a dog and those who dropped to their knees to drink. Whatever the purpose of the test, only three hundred soldiers were selected for Gideon's army.

Next God instructed Gideon to go with his servant Phurah down to the perimeter of the Midianite encampment and eavesdrop on the Midianites. They overheard one soldier telling another of his dream about a cake of barley bread that rolled into the Midian camp against the king's tent and flattened it. His fellow soldier interpreted the dream that this was none other than the sword of Gideon and that God was about to deliver Midian into Gideon's hands. So evident was it that this dream and the interpretation had both come from God that Gideon immediately returned to the host of Israel and said, "Arise; for the LORD hath delivered into your hand the host of Midian." Three hundred men defeated the entire Midianite army and the glory belonged entirely to God.

We must never shy away from impossible situations. When the odds seem least favorable for our success, that is when God can gain the greatest glory from our success. Large armies are not as admirable as dedicated ones. The recruiting slogan of the United States Marine Corps is "A few good men." God is looking for the same. Will you be one today?

MORNING HYMN

> *On ev'ry hand the foe we find*
> *Drawn up in dread array;*
> *Let tents of ease be left behind,*
> *And onward to the fray!*
> *Salvation's helmet on each head,*
> *With truth all girt about:*
> *The earth shall tremble 'neath our tread*
> *And echo with our shout.*

Morning Moments

MORNING SCRIPTURE   Psalm 119:129-152
MORNING VERSE   Psalm 119:147

I prevented the dawning of the morning, and cried; I hoped in Thy word.

TODAY our early morning devotional takes us to the great psalm—Psalm 119. This is a psalm dedicated to the praise of God's Word. It is the longest and most elaborate of the alphabetic psalms. While there are eight other acrostic psalms (9; 10; 25; 34; 37; 111; 112; and 145), this one far exceeds all the others in splendor. It is arranged in twenty-two stanzas, corresponding to the twenty-two letters in the Hebrew alphabet. Within each stanza the first line of every verse begins with the same letter in the Hebrew alphabet. Although we cannot see that in English, in our Bible the word supplied at the head of each stanza is the name of the Hebrew letter with which each verse in that stanza begins.

The author of the psalm is unknown but it is definitely Davidic in tone and expression and squares with David's experiences at many interesting points.

While these details of the psalm are interesting, devotionally there is something far more important in Psalm 119. The Masseretes, those scribes who copied the ancient Hebrew manuscripts of the Old Testament, observed that in every verse but one (verse 122) there is a direct reference to the law under one of ten legal names found in the psalm. Others dispute that claim but it is clear that the theme of this great psalm is the Word of God. The great preponderance of verses contain at least one word which identifies the Word of God and sings man's praises to it.

Psalm 119 is filled with delightful expressions of appreciation for God's Word. "Wherewithal shall a young man cleanse his way? By taking heed thereto according to Thy word" (verse 9). "I have rejoiced in the way of Thy testimonies, as much as in all riches" (verse 14). "I will speak of Thy testimonies also before kings, and will not be ashamed" (verse 46). "For ever, O LORD, Thy word is settled in heaven" (verse 89). "Thy word is a lamp unto my feet, and a light unto my path" (verse 105). With expressions of love and devotion like these, what more could God hear that would bring joy to His ears? What promise could the psalmist make that would seal his eagerness to know God's law?

Psalm 119:147 provides the answer. The psalmist says, "I prevented the *dawning of the morning*, and cried; I hoped in Thy word." Before the light broke through the shadows of the dark night, the psalmist was already prevailing on God in prayer. He cried unto His God before He spoke unto his fellow man. He spent time hoping in God's Word each morning before he gave himself to speaking God's Word throughout the day. It was at the dawning of the morning that the psalmist found the Word of God most precious to him.

Ambrose commented, "It is a grievous thing if the rays of the rising sun find thee lazy and ashamed in thy bed, and the bright light strike on eyes still weighed down with slumbering sloth." The psalmist would agree with this church father.

To delight in the law of God, to sing praises to the Word of God, to read and meditate on the testimonies of God, all bring joy to the heart of God. But I believe the greatest joy is brought to His heart when we do these things at the dawning of the day. When we seek His word above all others, His encouragement before all others, His truth instead of all others, then we will be pleasing to Him more than all others.

One grand benefit of preceding the dawn with Bible reading and prayer is that it will not only add God's blessing to our day, but it will also encourage us to continue in His Word and prayer throughout the day. The same psalmist who rose early in the morning to hope in God's Word continued into the night watches meditating in that same Word (verse 148). When we begin the day early in prayer and the Word, we can continue that practice throughout the day. But if we do not come to the Lord until the evening hours, we can never know the joy of spending the day with Him. Let us enjoy His Word throughout this day.

MORNING HYMN

> *Break Thou the bread of life,*
> *Dear Lord, to me,*
> *As Thou didst break the loaves*
> *Beside the sea;*
> *Beyond the sacred page*
> *I seek Thee, Lord;*
> *My spirit pants for Thee,*
> *O living Word.*

Come and Dine

MORNING SCRIPTURE   *John 21:1-25*
MORNING VERSE   *John 21:4*

But when the morning was now come, Jesus stood on the shore: but the disciples knew not that it was Jesus.

H AVE YOU ever noticed that the most difficult time to serve the Lord is immediately after a defeat in your life? When we are on a spiritual high, serving the Lord comes almost naturally. But when we experience the roller-coaster ride to the depths of despair after some spiritual tragedy we have a tendency to become complacent. While activity tends to produce additional activity, inactivity also reproduces itself.

The popularity of Jesus Christ had been building throughout His earthly ministry. Thousands of people followed Him through the hills of Galilee, watching His miracles and listening to His teachings. The disciples had become an intimate group, well known for their association with Jesus. As His popularity grew, so did their own.

The culmination of their intimate relationship with the Lord came the night of His betrayal. He had gathered the disciples in the upper room to keep the Passover. They were all there. They ate with the Lord, prayed with Him, sang hymns with Him, pledged their loyalty to Him. Around this meal, the institution of the Lord's supper, the disciples reached a spiritual high. Their heightened spirits, however, were soon to be dashed. Jesus was led away from the garden, He endured a cruel and illegal trial, and the disciples were dispersed. Even though Jesus again and again had told them that He must suffer the cruelty of the cross, the disciples still did not assimilate this tenet of His teaching. With His death and burial the disciples' balloon had burst. Even the resurrection of the Lord and the immediate post-resurrection appearances did not do much to reassure the disciples.

As instructed by the Lord Himself, the disciples returned to Galilee. Their meeting with Jesus on the mountain of Galilee where He had appointed them must have been subsequent to the account of our Scripture for today. Seven of the apostles had returned to their vocation as fishermen. How easy it was to be a follower of the Lord when He was present; how easy it was to return to their occupation in His absence.

It was Peter who first suggested that he would go fishing. This does not necessarily imply that he intended to renounce his apostleship in favor of the fishing trade. This is what he knew best; this is what he would do until the Lord commanded him otherwise. Hence Peter and the others entered into a ship and fished all night, but caught nothing. How could this be? Had they lost the knack of fishing during their years with the Messiah? Why were they so unsuccessful at a business in which they had been extremely successful before Jesus called them to discipleship? Throughout the night they fished without any success at all.

"But when *the morning was now come,* Jesus stood on the shore" (John 21:4). For some providential reason the disciples did not recognize the stranger standing on the shore. As He called to them inquiring how successful they had been, they had to answer that they were extremely unsuccessful in fishing that night. They did not recognize that it was the resurrected Lord keeping His rendezvous with them in Galilee until He commanded them to cast their nets on the other side of the ship. This was reminiscent of a similar but earlier command of the Lord with the same result (Luke 5:1-11).

When the disciples hauled in an incredible amount of fish, they came to the shore at Jesus' invitation to "Come and dine" (John 21:12). It was almost as if the Lord was reigniting the fire of intimacy and love which had cooled since their last supper together. Jesus Christ did not want His disciple band to become complacent, for complacency is kin to disobedience.

After we have once served the Lord well and lived in intimate relationship with Him, it is easy to become complacent, to drift from Him, and not to sit at His table. However, the Lord calls to each of us to "come and dine" and if we are to be an effective and useful tool in the Master's hand we must find our feet under His table frequently.

MORNING HYMN

> *Revive us again—fill each heart with Thy love;*
> *May each soul be rekindled with fire from above.*
> *Hallelujah, Thine the glory!*
> *Hallelujah, amen!*
> *Hallelujah, Thine the glory!*
> *Revive us again.*

Little Things

MORNING SCRIPTURE   1 Samuel 17:1-27
MORNING VERSE   1 Samuel 17:20

And David rose up early in the morning, and left the sheep with a keeper, and took, and went, as Jesse had commanded him; and he came to the trench, as the host was going forth to the fight, and shouted for the battle.

OCCASIONALLY it is necessary to remind ourselves that success in life often depends upon little things. Little people, little tasks, and little responsibilities often loom large in the eyes of God.

The Philistines waged frequent raids on Israel. The leader of the Philistines, a giant of tremendous stature named Goliath of Gath, was probably one of the Anakim (Numbers 13:33; Joshua 11:22), a strain of huge men that Joshua drove out of Hebron, and who took refuge among the Philistines. No Israelite was a match for Goliath, especially not little David who was sent to the battlefield to inquire of the welfare of his three elder brothers, Eliab, Abinadab, and Shammah. David's task was a small one; he was entrusted with very little. Told to take his brothers an ephah of parched corn and ten loaves, along with ten cheeses for the captain of the army, David set out to the battlefield. This day began with a small task, but it was to be a most momentous day in the history of Israel.

"David *rose up early in the morning,* and left his sheep with a keeper" and engaged in the small chore his father had commissioned to him (1 Samuel 17:20). As he talked with his brothers, behold the Philistine champion came out again to challenge the Israelites. The armies of Israel stood by trembling in their sandals, but David was appalled and amazed at the fear which paralyzed the Israelite warriors. Not willing to see his nation shamed or his God embarrassed, he inquired why someone did not stand up to the godless Goliath. "Who is this uncircumcised Philistine, that he should defy the armies of the living God?" Immediately his eldest brother whisked him away to quiet him. Someone entrusted with such a small task as bringing bread and cheese to his soldier-brothers should not be so vocal about the cowardice of the Israelite army.

Yes, David had slain the lion and the bear, but he was still slight in the sight of those around him. Those were but small feats; silencing the giant Goliath would be a gargantuan task. Besides, even if David accepted the challenge, he was too small to wear the armor necessary to enter battle with Goliath. His weapon, a sling, was likewise a small implement. Everything about David was small, including his chances of success against the giant. But as we all know, David's God was victorious; the slight shepherd of Israel slew the giant Goliath.

Horatius Bonar, reflecting on God using that which is small, realized that little things can frequently be used of God to be great things. He wrote, "A holy life is made up of a multitude of small things. It is the little things of the hour and not the great things of the age that fill up a life like that of the Apostle Paul or John, or David Brainard, or Henry Martyn. Little words not eloquent speeches or sermons, little deeds not miracles or battles, or one great heroic effort or martyrdom, make up the true Christian life. It's the little constant sunbeam, not the lightning, the waters of Siloam that go softly in their meek mission of refreshment, not the waters of the rivers great and main rushing down in torrent, noise, and force that are the true symbols of the holy life."

There are no small people, small tasks, or small responsibilities in the service of God. You can be small only if you fail to take the bread and cheese as God has commanded. How much happier Goliath would have been if little David had stayed home that day.

MORNING HYMN

> *Little is much, when God is in it!*
> *Labor not for wealth or fame;*
> *There's a crown—and you can win it,*
> *If you'll go in Jesus' name.*

Praising God

MORNING SCRIPTURE   1 *Chronicles* 23:1-32
MORNING VERSE   1 *Chronicles* 23:30

And to stand every morning to thank and praise the LORD, and likewise at even.

K ING DAVID, who himself had been a fugitive and a wanderer for many years of his life, would have liked nothing better than to build a permanent dwelling place for the ark of the covenant. But because he was a man of war, Jehovah would not permit David to realize this privilege, so David "called for Solomon his son, and charged him to build an house to the LORD God of Israel" (1 Chronicles 22:6). The zealous David did all he could to help in the preparations for the building of this Temple. He gathered materials, prepared iron for nails, and had a crew of masons readied. But an even greater contribution than arranging for the materials may have been David's initiation of the first full choral service. In conjunction with the chief of the Levites, David set apart three families and commissioned them to the service of the Temple. These were not just singers but prophets as well, "to prophesy with harps, with psalteries, and with cymbals" (1 Chronicles 25:1). Generation after generation their instruction was handed down from father to son and their art and musical skill was carefully perpetuated.

These families were those of Asaph, the son of Berechiah the Gershonite, the chief singer and also a distinguished seer; of Heman the Kohathite, the grandson of the prophet Samuel and himself, "the king's seer in the words of God" (1 Chronicles 25:5); and of Jeduthun (or Ethan), a Merarite, who is also called "the king's seer." Each of the names of these leaders is found in the titles or superscriptions of selected psalms in the Psalter.

From 1 Chronicles 23-25 we learn that the numbers of Levites involved in the service of the Temple and Tabernacle was enormous. The three families numbered two hundred eighty-eight principal singers, divided into twenty-four courses of twelve each. The total number of Levites engaged in the important task of praising Jehovah with the instruments which David made was four thousand. Six thousand were designated as officers and judges, four thousand were set apart to be doorkeepers, and the remaining twenty-four thousand Levites were designated to the general "work of the house of Jehovah."

Although to us their work may appear to be mundane, it certainly was not to them. They were to wait on the priests for the service of the house of Jehovah, purifying the holy place and the holy things, preparing the shewbread and the meat offering, and assisting in the offering of burnt sacrifices on the sabbaths and on feast days. But perhaps their greatest duty, as well as their greatest delight, was to stand *every morning* to thank and praise the Lord and likewise at even" (1 Chronicles 23:30).

Rising early in the morning these Levites would initiate the praise to Jehovah that day. This was not only a responsible position but a very meaningful one as well. Psalm 88, a psalm for the sons of Korah designated as a Maschil of Heman, gives a fine example of what these Levites may have said morning after morning in praising Jehovah. "But unto Thee have I cried, O LORD; and in the morning shall my prayer prevent [come before] Thee" (Psalm 88:13).

Rising early in the morning to initiate a day filled with praise to God is our privilege as well. May we be as faithful in exercising that privilege as David's choirmasters were. Faithfulness in early praise to God may make the difference between a good day and a bad day.

MORNING HYMN

> *Holy, Holy, Holy, Lord God Almighty!*
> *Early in the morning our song shall rise to Thee;*
> *Holy, Holy, Holy! Merciful and Mighty!*
> *God in Three Persons, blessed Trinity!*

Believing Is Not Seeing

MORNING SCRIPTURE   *Isaiah 37:1-38*
MORNING VERSE   *Isaiah 37:36*

Then the angel of the LORD went forth, and smote in the camp of the Assyrians a hundred and fourscore and five thousand: and when they arose early in the morning, behold, they were all dead corpses.

"N OW FAITH is the substance of things hoped for, the evidence of things not seen" (Hebrews 11:1). Perhaps no more graphic illustration of this truth can be found in the Scriptures than the events recorded in Isaiah 36 and 37. The Assyrian king, Sennacherib, had opened a campaign against Judah by attacking the fortresses in her southland. He was engaged in the seige of Lachish, a city southwest of Jerusalem, when he decided to send a contingent of soldiers against Jerusalem under Rabshakeh, his chief cupbearer. Apparently the Assyrians felt that King Hezekiah would surrender Jerusalem without a fight if Rabshakeh could dishearten the Jewish warriors.

The Assyrian cupbearer made light of Judah's possibilities of victory. Would she rely on the armies of the Pharaoh of Egypt, armies now so weakened that they are likened to leaning on a broken staff? Would she rely on the God of Israel in the face of the might of Assyria? What would Hezekiah and his Israelites do? The servants of King Hezekiah came to seek advice from Isaiah, the man of God. Isaiah assured Hezekiah that God took the blasphemies of Rabshakeh as uttered against Him personally and would destroy the armies of Sennacherib because of their blasphemy. In destroying the armies of the Assyrians the whole world would know "that Thou art the LORD, even Thou only" (Isaiah 37:20). Isaiah predicted that the king of Assyria would never enter God's holy city nor shoot an arrow at it. God would somehow miraculously deliver His city because of the blasphemy of the Assyrians against Him. Hezekiah and the Jews must live lives of faith for they would not be told how this deliverance would come about; they must trust God.

That very night the predicted catastrophe for the Assyrian armies occurred. "Then the angel of the LORD went forth and smote in the camp of the Assyrians a hundred and fourscore and five thousand: and when they arose *early in the morning*, behold, they were all dead corpses" (Isaiah 37:36). God had kept His word, even though the Jews could not see through the fog of doubt. Early in the morning they arose to find one hundred eighty-five thousand Assyrian corpses. They never had opportunity to move against God's holy city because God always performs what He promises.

On July 4, 1952, Florence Chadwick attempted to swim from Catalina Island to the California coast. It was not the distance that was the great challenge to her but the bone-chilling waters of the Pacific. To make matters worse, a dense fog enshrouded the entire area, making it impossible to see the land. After she had swum for fifteen hours and was within half a mile of her goal, Florence Chadwick gave up. Later she told a newspaper reporter, "If I could have seen land, I might have made it."

Not long thereafter she again attempted this same feat. Once again the fog shrouded the coastline and she could not see the shore, but this time she successfully completed her swim because she kept reminding herself that the land was out there, somewhere. With that confidence she bravely swam on and achieved her goal. In fact, she broke the men's record by more than two hours.

Sometimes we do not achieve our goals in life because we cannot clearly see God's hand moving in our behalf. Although we desire with all our heart to reach our goal, the fog of doubt sets in and makes it impossible for us to see clearly. Still, if believing in God we continue to press toward the mark, early in the morning we will see our goal achieved and the battlefield littered with the corpses of the enemy. We must trust God in the dark; we must remember that faith is the evidence of things not seen.

MORNING HYMN

> *O for a faith that will not shrink*
> *Tho pressed by many a foe,*
> *That will not tremble on the brink*
> *Of any earthly woe.*

Joy in the Morning

MORNING SCRIPTURE   Psalm 30:1-12
MORNING VERSE   Psalm 30:5

For His anger endureth but a moment; in His favour is life: weeping may endure for a night, but joy cometh in the morning.

L IKE in so many other psalms, in Psalm 30 David promises to praise the Lord. He had experienced a great deliverance and was thankful. He cried unto Heaven and the Lord heard him, bringing his soul back from the grave. Thus he exclaims that he will "Sing unto the Lord . . . for His anger endureth but a moment." This thought is reinforced by the delightful expression, "Weeping may endure for a night, but joy cometh *in the morning*" (Psalm 30:5).

How often have we experienced the truth of this verse! Heavy trials weigh us down as we pillow our heads at night. Our minds seem unable to bear the pressure. Restlessly we toss and turn, but our body refuses to rest. We are miserable and feel helpless. Finally sleep comes, but only after hours of restlessness.

The Christian life is filled with the interchanges of sickness and health, weakness and strength, disgrace and honor, want and wealth. Sometimes we enjoy the comfort of being one of God's own; other times we bear the cross of that same privilege. On occasion the south winds of God's mercy blow over our lives; on other occasions blow the north winds of adversity. Nonetheless, when the nipping north winds of calamity chill our nights and cause us to be restless, we may rest in the promise of God that "weeping may endure [only] for a night." God always places a time limit on the suffering and restlessness of His children.

After such a night of struggle, we frequently awake with a vague sense of what transpired the night before. As we gather our thoughts, we wonder why it was so difficult for us to fall asleep. Why were we so helpless and despairing? Things do not look as impossible as they once did. What is it that makes the difference? It is the joy which comes in the morning when we cast our care upon the Lord knowing that He cares for us (1 Peter 5:7 cf. Job 33:26; Isaiah 26:20; 54:7).

Not only are the trials of the night temporary; they are gift from God as well. We cannot deny that Christians are often called to endure soul-shaking experiences. In the Christian life there is weeping, and sometimes plenty of it. The nights of adversity are long and frequent. But God never allows them to be endless or without cause.

The cupola of St. Paul's Cathedral in London was painted by Sir James Thornhill. It was necessary for Sir James to complete his work while standing on a swinging scaffold high above the pavement. One day when he had finished a particularly difficult portion with painstaking effort, he stopped to inspect his artistry. As a good artist does, slowly he began moving backwards in order to gain a more appropriate view of his work. A helper working with him suddenly recognized that Sir James, should he take one step further backward, would be killed in a fatal fall. The man knew that if he startled the man with a shout it might topple him from the scaffold. Thus, as quickly as possible, he grabbed a brush and made a sweeping stroke across the exquisite work that Sir James was admiring. Understandably disturbed, the artist rushed forward with a cry of dismay. When his companion explained why he had taken this drastic measure, Sir James Thornhill burst into tears of gratitude.

We may be sure that no physician ever weighed out medicine to his patients with half as much care and exactness as God weighs out the trials of a sleepless night to us. Perhaps the dawning light of relief seems far away for you, but remember, morning will come, and with it God's promised joy. You have God's Word on it.

MORNING HYMN

> *Does Jesus care when my heart is pained*
> *Too deeply for mirth and song;*
> *As the burdens press, and the cares distress,*
> *And the day grows weary and long?*
> *O yes, He cares; I know He cares,*
> *His heart is touched with my grief;*
> *When the days are weary, the long nights dreary,*
> *I know my Saviour cares.*

Web of Conspiracy

MORNING SCRIPTURE   *Judges 9:22-57*
MORNING VERSE   *Judges 9:33*

And it shall be, that in the morning, as soon as the sun is up, thou shalt rise early, and set upon the city: and, behold, when he and the people that is with him come out against thee, then mayest thou do to them as thou shalt find occasion.

"OH WHAT a tangled web we weave, when first we practice to deceive." Conspirators against those who are righteous are ultimately destroyed by their conspiracy. How this is evident in the tragic days following the triumph of Gideon and his three hundred men.

Judges 8:33-35 records the failure of the Israelites to live after the defeat of the Midianites as they had during the battle. As a result of Israel's forgetting the God who delivered them, internal strife became more damaging than their external enemies. The royalty which Gideon had refused was coveted by Abimelech, his son by a handmaiden of Shechem. Attempting to trade on his father's reputation, Abimelech harangued the men of Shechem, claiming that it was far better to be ruled by one man, a Shechemite, than by all seventy of Gideon's sons. With money stolen from the sacred treasury of Baal-berith, Abimelech hired "vain and light persons," a band of desperadoes, to slay Gideon's other sons. Miraculously, however, one son, Jotham, escaped the conspiracy.

Abimelech reigned over a limited area in Israel for three years. But his reign did not go unchallenged by Jotham, who fled to Mount Gerizim where he pronounced a curse on Abimelech and the men of Shechem. This curse came in the form of a parable about the tree which wished one of their number to rule over them. They asked the olive tree, fig tree, and vine in succession, only to be rebuffed each time. Then they turned to the worthless thorny bramble, which accepted their offer to rule over them.

The meaning of this parable was obvious to all. The trees, which are themselves producers, are more interested in fruit than in control; but the thorn, which has nothing to give, seeks to be the leader sheerly for personal gain. Abimelech was a thorn. Jotham cried, "Let fire come out from Abimelech and devour the men of Shechem, and the house of Millo; and let fire come out from the men of Shechem, and from the house of Millo, and devour Abimelech" (Judges 9:20).

Jotham's curse was not long in being fulfilled. After three years God sent an "evil spirit" between Abimelech and the men of Shechem. The Shechemites revolted and plotted against his life. But Zebul, the governor of the city and an Abimelech loyalist, informed Abimelech of the plot to dethrone him and a counter plan was hatched. Zebul counseled Abimelech and his men to lie in wait for the Shechemites during the night in the fields before the city. "And it shall be, that *in the morning*, as soon as the sun is up, *thou shalt rise early* and set upon the city" (Judges 9:33). Abimelech massacred the inhabitants of Shechem.

Having treacherously murdered his pseudosubjects, Abimelech turned his attention to the neighboring city of Thebez. As some of the Shechemites, the men and women of Thebez fled to a strong tower for safety. Again Abimelech prepared to burn them out when a woman cast a piece of millstone out of the tower. In ironic reciprocation, the stone found its target—the head of Abimelech—and broke his skull. Jotham's prophecy was fulfilled.

Abimelech, the would-be-king conspirator, and the Shechemites, his would-be subjects, were caught in the middle of their web of conspiracy. Having destroyed the righteous, they were themselves destroyed by each other. Deception always brings destruction. How much better we are passively to accept the will of God as good, acceptable, and perfect (Romans 12:2) than to conspire self-promotion without the blessing of God.

MORNING HYMN

> The God of Abraham praise,
>   Who reigns enthroned above,
> Ancient of everlasting days,
>   And God of love.
> Jehovah, great I AM,
>   By earth and Heav'n confessed,
> I bow and bless the sacred
>   Name forever blest.

God Alone

MORNING SCRIPTURE   *Job 7:1-21*
MORNING VERSE   *Job 7:4*

When I lie down, I say, When shall I arise, and the night be gone? And I am full of tossings to and fro unto the dawning of the day.

T HE BOOK OF JOB is an epic poem ranking among the greatest writings of mankind. Alfred Lord Tennyson said that the book of Job was "the greatest poem of ancient or modern times." As the story of a man who lived righteously before God, was fiercely attacked by Satan, continued his righteous life, and had restored to him all that he lost and more, Job ought to be an encouragement to all of us. Somewhere in the book you and I find ourselves.

It was not bad enough that Job was attacked by Satan, but his three friends, who sought to comfort him, were equally vicious in their pompous assumptions about Job's sin. The majority of Job's chapters record cycles of speeches given by Job's friends and the replies of the righteous Job.

The first cycle contains the speech of Eliphaz. In vivid language, Eliphaz describes a vision in which he saw the majestic purity of God compared with the sinfulness of all of God's creative beings. Since only the evil perish, Job was experiencing his difficulty because he was evil, Eliphaz thought. His suggestion was that the righteous Job not be bitter but turn to God in repentance.

In replying to Eliphaz, Job likens human life to service in the armed forces, to the life of a hireling, to the lowly lot of a servant. Job can identify with each of these roles for he too is caught in a life situation well beyond his control. He recognizes that the servant or hireling has but a few days on earth and many of these days are lived in menial meaninglessness. Job feels the same way about his life, now that his family and possessions are gone and his friends have turned against him, assuming his unrighteousness.

I suppose each of us has had occasion to identify with Job 7:4. When Job lies upon his bed at night, and sleep does not come, his only thought is, "When shall I arise, and the night be gone?" When financial reversals or personal loss plague us and faithful friends fail us, the nights do seem long indeed. Like Job, we may feel that we are "full of tossings to and fro *until the dawning of the day*" (Job 7:4).

What can Job do? Where can he turn? Who is the one person who will listen and understand? In the transitoriness of life, who remains the same and forever? Job knows the answer; he will make his prayer to God and there find his hope.

Vance Havner once told a story about an elderly woman who was disturbed by her great and many troubles. Some of these troubles were real, others were but imaginary. After friends and family had prayed with her, comforted her, and attempted to help her, they reminded her, "Grandma, we've done all we can for you. You'll just have to trust God for the rest." With a look of shock and despair Grandma's eyes flashed back to her family the message, "Oh dear, has it come to that?" Havner notes, "It always comes to that, so we might as well begin with that!"

This is the lesson that Job learned. Sometimes in attempting to provide comfort, our family and friends actually do a disservice to our need. Sometimes we are misunderstood for our actions. But God always understands and God is always a source of comfort. It always comes to the need of resting in God. We may rest in Him for our health and strength, for vindication from false accusations, for companionship in time of solitude. It always comes to that and thank God it does.

MORNING HYMN

> *When peace, like a river, attendeth my way,*
> *When sorrows like sea billows roll—*
> *Whatever my lot, Thou hast taught me to say,*
> *It is well, it is well with my soul.*

Failure and Success

MORNING SCRIPTURE   *Joshua 8:1-35*
MORNING VERSE   *Joshua 8:10*

And Joshua rose up early in the morning, and numbered the people, and went up, he and the elders of Israel, before the people of Ai.

I T HAS BEEN aptly said that failure is the back door to success. Nowhere is this adage more graphically illustrated in Scripture than in the capture of Ai. With a task force of three thousand men, Israel had failed miserably in her attempted conquest of Ai because of one man's sin. Achan kept God's people from victory, but once his sin had been dealt with, victory would most assuredly come again to Israel.

The defeat at Ai could have dealt a devastating blow to Joshua's leadership. Joshua feared the Canaanites would hear of Israel's cowardice and their name would be cut off from the earth. His concern really was what such a defeat would mean to the great name of Jehovah God. But his fears were alleviated when Jehovah promised Joshua victory in the second battle of Ai.

The plan of attack for this battle, unlike that of Jericho, was far more likely to be included in military manuals. God told Joshua to put an ambush of thirty thousand men between Ai and Bethel to the west. To this was later added another ambush of five thousand men in the same direction. Meanwhile, "Joshua *rose up early in the morning*, and numbered the people, and went up, he and the elders of Israel, before the people of Ai" (Joshua 8:10). When the king of Ai saw what was happening, he too "hasted and *rose up early*" in the morning (Joshua 8:14). Mustering his Aiite troops, they marched out to meet the main body of the Israelite forces. Because the enemy was fully aware that Israel had retreated once in defeat, Joshua feigned a retreat, drawing his troops back to the northeast. The Aiite troops followed.

While this was happening, the Israelites waiting in ambush entered the now empty city of Ai and burned it to the ground. When the king and his men turned to see their city smoldering, they realized their defeat was imminent. They were surrounded by Israelite soldiers. The Israelites in the ambush then came out of

Ai and marched on the rear flank of the Aiite army. Joshua reversed his movement and caught the king and his men in a pincer movement. The people of Ai were defeated; Joshua's victory was now complete.

Joshua had taken the stumbling stone of defeat and turned it into the stepping-stone of success. In doing so he learned the valuable lesson that our greatest glory consists not in never failing, but in rising every time we fall. Others give striking testimony to this fact as well.

In 1832 a young American was a candidate for the legislature. He lost. In 1834 he was again a candidate and this time won. In 1847 he went to the United States Congress but served only one term. He wasn't even renominated by his party. He campaigned for Zachary Taylor for president, hoping to be appointed commissioner of the General Land Office. He wasn't. He returned to private law practice. In 1854 he again ran for the legislature and won but soon resigned because he hoped the new anti-Nebraska party would support him for the senate. They didn't. In 1856 he was nominated for the office of vice-president of the United States and lost. In 1858 he ran again for United States senate and lost again. In 1860 he was simply nominated as a favorite son from Illinois for the presidency—and later that year he, Abraham Lincoln, was elected president of the United States. Like Lincoln, we must never allow yesterday's mistakes to bankrupt tomorrow's efforts.

Just as there is no failure more disastrous than success that leaves God out of the picture, likewise there is no success greater than the rediscovery of the power of God in our life. We must never be ashamed to confess that we have failed, for this is but one way of saying we are wiser today than we were yesterday.

MORNING HYMN

> *Immortal, invisible, God only wise,*
> *In light inaccessible hid from our eyes,*
> *Most blessed, most glorious, the Ancient of Days,*
> *Almighty, victorious—Thy great name we praise.*

The Deceitful Heart

MORNING SCRIPTURE   Exodus 32:1-35
MORNING VERSE   Exodus 32:6

And they rose up early on the morrow, and offered burnt offerings, and brought peace offerings; and the people sat down to eat and to drink, and rose up to play.

THE PROPHET JEREMIAH observed that, "The heart is deceitful above all things, and desperately wicked; who can know it?" (Jeremiah 17:9). The Bible gives more than ample evidence to support Jeremiah's observation. In fact, so does this morning's newspaper.

A prime example of how innately wicked the human heart is can be seen in the unfaithfulness of Israel at Mount Sinai. When the people of God encamped at the foot of the mountain, Moses ascended the slopes of Sinai and received the Law. After the people acknowledged the covenant of God and answered with one voice, "All the words which the LORD hath said will we do" (Exodus 24:3), Moses again ascended the mount of God. This time he received God's instruction in the ordinances of divine worship.

Moses' sojourn on the mountain was much longer than anyone expected. After nearly six weeks passed without his return, the people grew impatient and fearful. Had they lost their leader? How could Moses survive on the mountain without food? And what about their God? He was on the mountain too, in the pillar of a cloud that led them from Egypt. Had He forsaken them?

Israel had come face to face with a real test of faith, a test they failed miserably. As long as Moses was with the Israelites he could encourage them to "live by faith and not by sight." But now he was gone and Israel's faith rapidly evaporated. The desperate wickedness of their hearts came to the fore. The Israelites frantically begged Aaron to make gods for them, gods that would go before them as the Everlasting God had done in the cloud. Immediately Aaron instructed the people to take off their golden earrings, which were then melted down and fashioned into an idolatrous golden calf. Aaron proclaimed that on the next day they would have a feast to the Lord.

The Israelites were like a child with a new toy, barely sleeping that night because of excitement. "And they *rose up early on the morrow,* and offered burnt offerings and brought peace offerings" (Exodus 32:6). The people then sat down to eat and drink. But the Bible says that after that they "rose up to play." This may sound innocent enough, but the "play" in which the people of God engaged was hardly the harmless kind. They fell into the pattern of sensuality that accompanies pagan worship. Idol worship nearly always ended in an orgy so disgusting that it cannot be described. So boisterous was the Israelite orgy that when Moses and Joshua returned from the mount, Joshua assumed the delirious shouts of the people were noises of war. But the people of God were caught up in a wild frenzy which was both licentious and idolatrous. It was the sight of this frenzy that angered Moses and caused him to cast the tables of stone to the ground, breaking them.

Exodus 32:25 enhances our understanding of the depths to which the Israelites had fallen. Not only were the people worshiping an idol, engaged in a wild orgy, and worked into a frenzy by licentious dancing, they were naked as well. Their nakedness was not only offensive to Moses but it was an affront to God as well.

There is scarcely a depth to which Satan cannot drag the desperately wicked human heart, even the hearts of God's chosen people. New Testament believers must never be deceived into thinking that we have sufficient strength in ourselves to keep us from similar depths of sin. Only the Spirit of God can prevent our wicked hearts from dragging us into sin. Today, let us pray as the Lord Jesus taught us, "And lead us not into temptation, but deliver us from evil" (Matthew 6:13).

MORNING HYMN

> *Search me, O God, and know my heart today;*
> *Try me, O Saviour, know my thoughts, I pray;*
> *See if there be some wicked way in me:*
> *Cleanse me from ev'ry sin, and set me free.*

Rewardable Service

MORNING SCRIPTURE   *Matthew 19:16–20:16*
MORNING VERSE   *Matthew 20:1*

For the kingdom of heaven is like unto a man that is an house-holder, which went out early in the morning to hire labourers into his vineyard.

JESUS' favorite method of teaching was by parable. A parable is an account which may or may not have actually happened but nonetheless is designed to teach a truth. One of our Lord's most difficult parables is the parable of the kingdom which is likened to a householder.

In summary the parable is this. *Early in the morning* one day a householder went out to hire laborers for a vineyard (Matthew 20:1). He agreed to pay the laborers a penny for the day, which was evidently the regular wages for the ordinary laborer. About the third hour the man returned to town and hired others to work in his vineyard, promising to pay them what was fair. At the sixth, ninth, and eleventh hours he returned to find others standing idle and likewise hired them with the same promise of payment.

At the end of the day, the householder called his laborers together and had the steward of the house pay them, beginning with the last hired. Each was paid the same, but when those who were hired early in the morning received just a penny they murmured that it was unfair to pay them a penny when those who had worked only an hour were also paid a penny. The householder replied that he had been just with the daylong workers, as he had been with the hourlong workers, and that whatever funds he had were his; he could do with them as he chose.

What would the Lord have us to learn about Him from this parable? There are three things.

First, the Lord Jesus seeks laborers for His vineyard. There is much work to be done if we are going to win the world for Christ and train those who have been won to reproduce themselves and bear fruit in abundance. We are not saved to sit, soak, and sour; we are saved to serve the Lord. The most frustrated person in the world, I believe, is not the unsaved person; he has little understanding of what really awaits him. The most frustrated person in the world is the one who is saved and does not know why God has left him on the earth. Ephesians 2:10 claims, "For we are His workmanship, created in Christ Jesus unto good works, which God hath before ordained that we should walk in them." The Lord saved us to be laborers in His field.

Secondly, the Lord Jesus hires laborers at various hours and various stages in life. The Church did not begin fully equipped. Throughout history others have been added to the New Testament Church, as we have been added during these last decades. Those who were apostles in the New Testament Church will not receive a greater wage for their labors simply because they entered early into Christ's vineyard. God is interested in rewardable labor, not the hour in which we became laborers. Should you have come to know the Lord as Saviour later in life and not have the opportunities to serve Him as those who have been saved many years, do not despair. God is absolutely just in meting out rewards.

Thirdly, the Lord Jesus rewards generously as well as justly. This final lesson that this parable teaches us is perhaps the greatest of all. Each of these laborers was rewarded in an unexpected manner. Each one received a penny, a day's wage, and no one could complain that he was paid less than fair wages. Beyond acting justly to those who had been hired first, the householder acted generously to the others. When people see generosity to others and not to themselves, they are hurt and accuse the generous person of being unfair. But this is not the case. Having rewarded justly, the Lord Jesus was then free to reward generously.

A kind storekeeper once said to a little girl who was eagerly eyeing a jar of candy, "Take some; take a whole handful!" The little girl hesitated for a moment and then replied, "Will you please give it to me? Your hand is bigger than mine!" When we begin to compare our lives with others and compute our anticipated rewards, we will be dissatisfied. What we must do is let the hand of God reward us as He deems just and fair. Remember, His hand is always bigger than ours. Let us live for Him today; let Him reward us tomorrow.

MORNING HYMN

> *Praise the Saviour, ye who know Him!*
> *Who can tell how much we owe Him?*
> *Gladly let us render to Him*
> *All we are and have.*

Jealousy

MORNING SCRIPTURE   1 Samuel 20:11-42
MORNING VERSE   1 Samuel 20:35

And it came to pass in the morning, that Jonathan went out into the field at the time appointed with David, and a little lad with him.

THE WISE SOLOMON once said, "Jealousy is cruel as the grave; its coals thereof are coals of fire" (Song of Solomon 8:6). The classic case of jealousy in the Bible is that of King Saul.

Young David had slain the giant Goliath and the women of the city responded by chanting, "Saul hath slain his thousands, and David his ten thousands" (1 Samuel 18:7). Hearing this displeased the king greatly. Saul was tormented by the thought that, although he was king over all Israel, yet the darling of the nation was David. Envy and jealousy, like a green-eyed monster, began to swallow him up.

No longer could David serve in the court of Saul, for twice Saul attempted to take his life. So David hid himself in the field and absented himself from the king's table. When the jealous Saul demanded of Jonathan the cause of David's absence, Jonathan's reply was that David had asked permission to attend a family feast at Bethlehem. But Saul saw this as merely an excuse and was enraged at his son. With the deepest insult possible to Jonathan, a slur with regard to his birth, Saul taunted the lad about his friendship with David. Ordered to fetch David so that Saul might kill him, Jonathan immediately reacted unfavorably and Saul hurled his javelin at his own son. Jonathan left the table in understandable anger.

"And it came to pass *in the morning*, that Jonathan went out into the field at the time appointed with David, and a little lad with him" (1 Samuel 20:35). Under the guise of target practice, Jonathan took the young lad to fetch his arrows as he shot them. This would prohibit Saul or anyone else being suspicious about why Jonathan was out in the field. When the young lad was dismissed, David emerged from his hiding place and the two lifelong friends renewed their covenant of friendship. Amid embraces and tears, they parted to meet again on only one brie occasion. This sad parting was occasioned by the jealousy of one man. Such jealousy removes the mind from reality and dethrones reason from its seat of judgment. The reins of reason are handed over to passion and the end result is illogical behavior.

D. L. Moody related a fable of an eagle who was envious of another bird that could fly better than he. One day the bird saw a sportsman with a bow and arrow and said to him, "I wish you would bring down that eagle up there." The man said he could do it if he only had some feathers for his arrow. So the jealous eagle pulled out one of his wing feathers. The man placed it on his arrow and shot at the flying eagle, but it did not quite reach the rival bird. The jealous eagle pulled out another feather, and another—until he had lost so many feathers that he could not fly himself. The wise archer then took advantage of the situation, simply turning around and killing the helpless bird at his side. Moody's application was simple: if you're envious of others, the one you will hurt the most will be yourself.

Saul's jealousy of David was his eventual undoing. Proverbs 14:30 says, "A sound heart is the life of the flesh; but envy the rottenness of the bones." We must never allow ourselves to fall prey to the monster within us, a monster that can arise on any occasion if we feed our jealousy.

MORNING HYMN

Would you live for Jesus and be always pure and good?
Would you walk with Him within the narrow road?
Would you have Him bear your burden, carry all your load?
Let Him have His way with thee.

Firm in Faith

MORNING SCRIPTURE   Mark 16:1-20
MORNING VERSE   Mark 16:2

And very early in the morning the first day of the week, they came unto the sepulchre at the rising of the sun.

FAITH is not always a champion which marches alone. Sometimes faith is accompanied by fear. Faith is not the absence of questioning; it is the presence of action in the midst of those questions. Faith does not provide all the answers; it provides a basis for confidence in the midst of unreasonable circumstances.

We do not fully understand how God takes oxygen and hydrogen, both of them odorless, tasteless, and colorless, and combines them with carbon, which is insoluble, black, and tasteless, to produce a beautiful, white, sweet substance we call sugar. Although we do not have all the answers as to how God accomplishes this, in the midst of our circumstances we accept God's product on faith. Real faith is "the substance of things hoped for, the evidence of things not seen" (Hebrews 11:1). Faith is trusting God when you cannot see through the fog.

It was early Easter Sunday morning when Mary Magdalene, Mary the mother of James, and Salome set out on a mission of faith. These women had covenanted among themselves to purchase spices that were needed to embalm the body of Jesus. They could not do so until after dusk on Saturday. So, when the Sabbath was passed, the women purchased the sweet spices that they might come to the tomb of Joseph and there make ready for burial the body of the Lord Jesus.

It was *very early in the morning* the first day of the week that they came to the sepulcher, *at the rising of the sun* (Mark 16:2). With the spices in hand that they had purchased the previous evening, the women made their way through the dark streets of Jerusalem just before the sunrise of Sunday morning. As they approached the garden in which the tomb was located, they chattered among themselves questioning how they would gain access to the tomb. Here is a grand example of faith amid questions. The women could not themselves roll away the stone for it was simply too cumbersome to do so. Yet they did not stay at home and attend a seminar on stone-rolling, argue the pros and cons of gaining entrance to the tomb, or form a committee to study the problem. In the midst of their concerns about how they would gain entrance to the tomb, they steadily progressed toward the tomb in faith. Faith is not the absence of questions; it is the presence of action amidst those questions.

Once an ocean liner was engulfed in a dense fog off the coast of Newfoundland. It was Wednesday evening and the captain had been on the bridge for more than twenty-four hours when he was startled by someone tapping him on the shoulder. As he turned he saw the great man of prayer and faith, George Mueller. The concerned Mueller stated, "Captain, I must be in Quebec on Saturday afternoon." Expressing his dismay the captain replied, "That's impossible!" The fog was so dense and the progress of the ship so slow that the captain knew they would never make it to shore on time. He mumbled, "I'm helpless!" Being a man of faith, George Mueller suggested, "Let's go down to the chart room and pray." The captain, who could see only his circumstances, replied, "Do you know how dense the fog is?"

"No," Mueller said, "My eye is not on the density of the fog, but on the living God who controls every circumstance of my life." The captain and Mueller left the bridge and went below where Mueller fell to his knees and prayed. Within a matter of minutes the fog lifted, the ocean liner progressed rapidly, and Mueller was in Quebec before Saturday.

If we are to live a life of faith we must get our eyes off the stone before the tomb and on the God who does the impossible. The women knew the stone would keep them from their Lord and yet they purchased their spices, readied themselves early in the morning, and made their way in the darkness toward the garden tomb. Faith is not being free from questions; faith is being firm in commitment to the power of God. How will you demonstrate your faith today?

MORNING HYMN

> *May Thy rich grace impart*
> *Strength to my fainting heart,*
> *My zeal inspire;*
> *As Thou hast died for me,*
> *O may my love to Thee*
> *Pure, warm and changeless be*
> *A living fire!*

Character

MORNING SCRIPTURE   *Psalm 73:1-28*
MORNING VERSE   *Psalm 73:14*

For all the day long have I been plagued, and chastened every morning.

T HIS IS THE SECOND psalm ascribed to Asaph, and the first of eleven consecutive psalms which bear his name. In 2 Chronicles 29:30 King Hezekiah invites the Levites to sing "the words of David, and of Asaph the seer." Asaph was not only a writer but a prophet as well. This psalm deals with the same perplexing subject as that of Psalm 37, curiously the transposition of Psalm 73. It is the subject of Psalm 49 and the entire book of Job. How can an infinitely powerful God be good and still allow the wicked to appear to prosper and the righteous to be in want? Perhaps you have asked the same question of God. If so, your answer is given in Psalm 73.

The way to Heaven is an afflicted way, a perplexed, a persecuted way, crushed close together with crosses as was the Israelites' way in the wilderness. This was true of Asaph the psalmist when his feet were almost gone and his steps had well nigh slipped. He was envious when he looked around him and saw the prosperity of the wicked. There were no pangs or pains in their death. The eyes of the wicked ever gloat on the luxuries around them. They increase in prosperity and riches while they curse God and the Almighty appears to do nothing about it.

On the other hand, Asaph had cleansed his heart and had washed his hands before God. He had lived uprightly and yet he was afflicted and distressed. Why would God allow him to be afflicted when he had lived as God desired? Although God does not daily bring a man to his bed, breaking his spirit and his bones, nevertheless seldom a day passes without some rebuke or chastening from God. It is as much a part of the Christian's life to know afflictions as it is to know mercies; to know when God smites as to know when He smiles.

Still Asaph complains, "For all day long have I been plagued, and chastened *every morning*" (Psalm 73:14). Every morning it appears to the psalmist that he arose after having been whipped by God. His breakfast was the bread of sorrow; his juice was the water of adversity. Morning after morning he would arise only to feel the affliction of God that day. Asaph began to question whether or not it was worth living a godly life, a life pure and unspotted from the world, when those around him refused to do so and prospered. Perhaps this question has crossed your mind as well.

In the forests of northern Europe lives the ermine, a small animal which we know best for its snow-white fur. Instinctively the ermine protects its white coat lest it become soiled. European hunters often capitalize on this trait. Instead of setting a mechanical trap to catch the ermine, they find its home in the cleft of a rock and daub the entrance with tar. A chase ensues and the frightened ermine flees toward its home. When it arrives at the cleft of the rock, finding it covered with dirt, the animal spurns its place of safety. Rather than soil itself and its white fur, it courageously faces the hunters. That's character. To the ermine, purity is dearer than life itself.

Whenever those occasions arise that we feel we are being chastised by God unjustly and we are tempted to cast off our righteous lifestyle, let's remember the ermine. To keep ourselves "unspotted from the world" (James 1:27) should be as important to the Christian as life itself. Affliction tests character and character tested, with the right response, is character strengthened. Rejoice today that God loves you enough to afflict you.

MORNING HYMN

> *In the hour of trial, Jesus, plead for me;*
> *Lest by base denial I depart from Thee;*
> *When Thou see'st me waver, with a look recall;*
> *Nor thro' fear or favor suffer me to fall.*

Betrayal

MORNING SCRIPTURE *Judges 16:1-31*
MORNING VERSE *Judges 16:2*

And it was told the Gazites, saying, Samson is come hither. And they compassed him in, and laid wait for him all night in the gate of the city, and were quiet all the night, saying, In the morning, when it is day, we shall kill him.

O F ALL THE JUDGES God raised up to steer Israel through the most stormy period of her history, none is as remarkable or pathetic as Samson. Like Samuel the priest, he was a son of much prayer. The announcement of Samson's birth to Manoah, his father, was made by an angel of the Lord. Judges 13:24 sums up the potential for God found in the life of Samson when it says, "And the child grew, and the LORD blessed him."

As he grew strong and tall, and kept to the restrictions of the Nazarite vow placed upon him (Judges 13:5), it soon became evident that this man was going to be a champion in Israel. Early the Spirit of the Lord began to move upon him (Judges 13:25). Three times during his early life the Scriptures note that "the Spirit of the Lord came mightily upon him" (Judges 14:6,19; 15:14). As long as Samson kept the razor from his head and pride from his heart, Samson would perform mightily for God.

There is evidence, however, that early in his life Samson began to enjoy his strength and stature. Although it was strictly forbidden of the Israelites to take wives of the Philistines, nonetheless Samson saw a Philistine woman of Timnath and said to his father, "Get her for me; for she pleaseth me well" (Judges 14:3). Samson's subsequent antics against the Philistines caused a committee of three thousand men of Judah to approach him and question, "Knowest thou not that the Philistines are rulers over us?" (Judges 15:11). But Samson was enjoying the might of the Spirit of the Lord and with the jawbone of an ass slew a thousand Philistines. He continued to judge Israel in the days of the Philistines for twenty years.

It was evident that something must be done to stop this Israelite strongman and the men of Gaza hatched a plan. When Samson went to a harlot of Gaza, one of his frequent and pathetic follies, the men of Gaza compassed him about, closed the city gate around him, and waited for an opportunity to kill him. They said, "*In the morning*, when it is day, we shall kill him" (Judges 16:2). But as before, their attempts were foiled when Samson arose at midnight, removed the doors of the city gate and carried them to the top of the hill alongside Hebron. This Philistine plan to kill Samson had failed; another would follow.

For the third and final time Samson would betray his people by an illicit relationship with a Philistine woman. The lords of the Philistines bribed Delilah to entice Samson to tell her the secret of his great strength. Three times he allowed himself to be bound with green withes or new ropes and to permit seven locks of his hair to be woven to the beam of a loom. Each time the treacherous Delilah would suddenly announce, "The Philistines be upon thee, Samson," and in human strength he would free himself to ward off the enemy. Samson appeared not to resent Delilah's evident treachery but rather to have enjoyed flaunting his strength before the Philistine lass. Finally, wearied by her persistence, Samson "told her all his heart" and confided to her the secret of his great strength. As he slept she cut his hair; his strength left him. The Philistines took him down to Gaza, bound him with fetters, put out his eyes, and caused him to grind grain in the prison house.

The story of the man upon whom the Spirit of the Lord came mightily could have been much different. It ended in tragedy because Samson displayed a total disregard for the laws of God with regard to the Philistines. He appeared to flaunt his God-given strength in a humanistic manner and continually to flirt with sin and disaster. Instead of fleeing the treacherous and deceitful Delilah, Samson tried to outwit and impress her. Perhaps the saddest comment of this sad life is found in Judges 16:20 where the writer notes of Samson, "He wist not that the LORD was departed from him."

We must recognize that our abilities and opportunities are truly gifts from God and we must use them mightily and wisely in the Spirit of the Lord. If we do not, like Samson, the world will make sport of us and our God.

MORNING HYMN

> *O how the world to evil allures me!*
> *O how my heart is tempted to sin!*
> *I must tell Jesus and He will help me*
> *Over the world the vict'ry to win.*

Foolish Vows

MORNING SCRIPTURE   *Genesis 44:1-17*
MORNING VERSE   *Genesis 44:3*

As soon as the morning was light, the men were sent away, they and their asses.

A WEATHERMAN, certain that his prediction for fair weather would be fulfilled, said, "If it rains tomorrow, I'll eat my hat!" Such a lightly considered vow is an invitation to disaster for it is entirely possible that factors unknown to the weatherman may cause a downpour. The Bible gives many similar examples of foolishly made oaths (cf. Judges 11).

During the worldwide seven years' famine in the days of Jacob, the sons of the patriarch found themselves trapped by such a foolish vow. They had sold their brother Joseph into slavery and unknown to them he had risen to a position of great authority in the Egyptian government. With the supply of grain in Canaan exhausted, Jacob sent his sons to Egypt to buy grain. In Pharaoh's land the brothers purchased grain from Joseph, whom they did not recognize. After that grain was gone, they returned to Egypt to buy more.

When they came to Joseph the second time he invited them to dine and commanded the steward to fill the men's sacks with food and put their purchase money back in each sack. Also Joseph specifically instructed that his silver cup be placed in the sack of the youngest brother, Benjamin. *"As soon as the morning was light"* the brothers embarked on the long trek back to Canaan (Genesis 44:3). Before they had gone very far Joseph commanded the steward to overtake them and accuse the brothers of stealing his royal cup. This was not done to be vindictive but simply to test the loyalty and integrity of the brothers who had once sold Joseph into slavery.

As soon as the charge was leveled against the sons of Jacob they indignantly denied it. To think that this steward would accuse them of dishonesty. In order to intensify their claim of innocence and fully unaware that Joseph had planted the cup in Benjamin's sack, the brothers hastily vowed a vow: "With whomsoever of thy servants it be found, both let him die, and we also will be my lord's servants." Suddenly they were trapped. They had made an irrevocable oath which would enslave them and bring death to their father's favorite son. When the search was made and the cup was found in Benjamin's sack, the brothers tore their clothes in anguish and returned to Joseph, the Egyptian governor.

It was no sin to vow this vow, for the making of such oaths was entirely voluntary. However, after a vow was made it was sacredly binding (Deuteronomy 23:21). The Apostle Paul called upon God in making an oath (2 Corinthians 1:23; 11:31) and our Lord Himself did not refuse to answer when put under oath (Matthew 26:63-64). Yet the Lord Jesus refined the general thought of Scripture on vowing vows when He said, "Swear not at all; neither by heaven . . . Nor by the earth. . . . Neither shalt thou swear by thy head. . . . But let your communication be, Yea, yea; Nay, nay; for whatsoever is more than these cometh of evil" (Matthew 5:34-37).

This does not mean that we cannot vow a vow to God. Rather, by the time of the New Testament the practice of making hasty and unmeaningful oaths was common. Oriental conversation was sprinkled with expressions like, "I swear that. . . ." This profaned the true meaning and sacred character of a vow and our Lord condemned the practice. Much better, said He, that others are assured that what you say is true by your personal integrity than by an unmeaningful oath.

It would be better to make no oath at all than to make one with no intention of keeping it (Ecclesiastes 5:5). Vows made with pure intentions and based on certain knowledge can bring great blessings. But those hastily made, like that of Jacob's sons, or those loosely used in ordinary conversation, are to be shunned by all who seek a life pleasing to God. Be careful what vows you make today! Be careful to keep those you have made!

MORNING HYMN

> *So shall my walk be close with God,*
> *Calm and serene my frame;*
> *So purer light shall mark the road*
> *That leads me to the Lamb.*

Mysterious Ways

MORNING SCRIPTURE   Numbers 22:1-35
MORNING VERSE   Numbers 22:13

And Balaam rose up in the morning, and said unto the princes of Balak, Get you into your land: for the LORD refuseth to give me leave to go with you.

THE FAMOUS English hymnist William Cowper once wrote, "God moves in mysterious ways His wonders to perform." Nowhere in the pages of Scripture is this more evident than in the story of Balak, the king of Moab, and Balaam, the false prophet of Pethor in Mesopotamia.

With the conquest of the Amorites, the people of Israel neared their goal, the promised land. They descended into the valley of Jordan opposite Jericho on the plains of Moab. Such a bold move by Israel aroused the Moabites. Seeing that Israel was too strong for him in the field, Moabite king Balak made a confederacy with the sheiks of Midian. But even the combined strength of Moab and Midian was of doubtful value in the face of mighty Israel. It was evident to Balak that supernatural help must be sought.

The prophet Balaam, son of Beor, was one of those who still retained some knowledge of the true God. It is obvious, however, that he practiced the more questionable arts of divination as well and in fact believed that Jehovah was simply one of many gods. He found it quite to his advantage to believe in all the gods of oriental society. The emissaries from Balak came to Balaam with a strange request. There was a people come out of Egypt who covered the face of the earth. They were a threat to the very existence of Moab, or so the Moabite king believed. If Balaam would curse the intruders, the emissaries were empowered to give him the rewards of divination.

Balaam consulted the God of Heaven as to the advisability of cursing the people who had come out of Egypt. The answer of Jehovah left no room for variant interpretations. "Thou shalt not go with them: thou shalt not curse the people: for they are blessed" (Numbers 22:12). Balaam *rose up in the morning* and reported to the princes of Balak that Jehovah had directly forbidden him to curse their enemy Israel.

When the princes returned to Balak with this unexpected news, the Moabite king was undaunted. He sent to Balaam more numerous and more honorable envoys. The king promised the prophet that he would promote him to very great honor and give him any desire of his heart. The greed of Balaam was too much for his loyalty to the God of Heaven and consequently he wavered in his stand against cursing Israel. Instead of resting confidently on the clear word of the Lord, Balaam hedged on that clarity in order to feed his lustful desire for fame and honor. Thus God gave him his desire and delivered him to the destruction that he courted. Despite the evident will of God to the contrary, Balaam *rose up in the morning,* and saddled his ass, and went with the princes of Moab" (Numbers 22:21).

This Old Testament account features the miraculous happening of a dumb animal speaking to his master in order that the plan of God might be fulfilled. But an even more mysterious way in which God moved to perform His wonders was that He chose a false prophet, one who thought more of himself than he did of God, to advance one of the greatest prophecies of the Old Testament. It was Balaam the son of Beor who brought the message of Christ in the book of Numbers. His messianic prophecy was, "I shall see Him, but not now: I shall behold Him, but not nigh: there shall come a Star out of Jacob and a Sceptre shall rise out of Israel, and shall smite the corners of Moab, and destroy all the children of Sheth" (Numbers 24:17).

No greater prophecy concerning the messianic kingdom can be found anywhere in Scripture and, in the mysterious plan of God, this prophecy came from the lips of a self-seeking prophet. We may never fully be able to understand the methods or motives of God, but we are not required to understand them, simply to trust them.

MORNING HYMN

> *Praise to the Lord,*
> *Who o'er all things so wondrously reigneth,*
> *Shelters thee under*
> *His wings, yea, so gently sustaineth!*
> *Hast thou not seen*
> *All that is needful hath been*
> *Granted in what He ordaineth?*

The Trial of Faith

MORNING SCRIPTURE   Job 24:1-25
MORNING VERSE   Job 24:14

*The murderer rising with the light killeth the poor and needy,
and in the night is as a thief.*

T HROUGHOUT Job's long ordeal, one concern continually raced
through his mind. He was fully aware that all men are
sinners and therefore are justly deserving of divine punishment. His concern was, however, that he had always dealt with
sin in an open manner. He had sacrificed daily to the Lord God
and had conducted his life in such a way that it was pleasing to
God. Throughout the ordeal the so-called comfort afforded him
by his three friends was generated by the belief that Job's suffering was the result of secret sin and that, if he would confess that
sin, God would surely remove the suffering. Job, however, knew
of no secret sin in his life and believed that his suffering must be
due to his piety. Job's mind was characterized by bewilderment,
not by the suppression of known sin.

Job's understanding of the foolish heart of man is theologically correct. He knows that sin can never be successfully hidden
from God. So wicked is the heart of man that he will confiscate
the property of the fatherless, deny charity to the poor, and as
wild asses *rising with the light* they kill the poor and needy assuming that no one will discover their crime (Job 24:14). *"The morning
is to them even as the shadow of death"* (Job 24:17) for the rising
of the sun brings to light the wickedness in which they have been
engaged throughout the dark hours of the night. Yet Job knows
that he has not conducted himself in this manner. It is understandable that God would punish with affliction those who have lived
in the way Job has described, but it is not understandable why
the righteous should suffer in the same manner. Job was upright
before the Lord; how could the Lord allow this to happen to him?

A similar circumstance once occurred in the life of William
Carey, the pioneer missionary to India. After his work was established, those who supported him in England sent a printer to
assist him in the work. Together they began producing portions of
the Bible for distribution in India. One day while he was away

from his station a fire broke out and completely destroyed everything Carey had accomplished. The building, the presses, the Bibles, and worst of all the manuscripts, grammars, and dictionaries on which he had spent many years of his life were all burned and destroyed. When Carey returned, his servant met him and tearfully relayed the news of the dreadful fire. How would Carey react? Without a word of despair or anger, William Carey knelt and thanked God that he still had strength enough to do that work all over again. Immediately he began, not wasting his time or licking his wounds. Before Carey died, under the direction of the Spirit of God he had not only duplicated his earlier achievements, but produced far better grammars, dictionaries, and translations of the Scripture than the first time.

William Carey had learned what Job had learned. Disaster does not necessarily mean the presence of secret sin. Sometimes God allows the pious to suffer just as He allows the impious. It is the trial of our faith that worketh patience and without this trial the legendary patience of Job would not be such a comfort to us today.

May each of us view those disasters that enter our lives through the godly glasses of courage and patience. May our lives be free from known sin so that with Job we may say of the Lord, "But He knoweth the way that I take: when He hath tried me, I shall come forth as gold" (Job 23:10).

MORNING HYMN

I would be true, for there are those who trust me;
I would be pure, for there are those who care;
I would be strong, for there is much to suffer;
I would be brave, for there is much to dare.

Morning Marching Orders

MORNING SCRIPTURE   *Psalm 143:1-12*
MORNING VERSE   *Psalm 143:8*

Cause me to hear Thy lovingkindness in the morning; for in Thee do I trust: cause me to know the way wherein I should walk; for I lift up my soul unto Thee.

I N TODAY'S modern, rushing world, many of us have all we can do to get out of bed in the morning and get to work on time. Often our schedule appears to preclude the possibility of morning devotions. Yet under the old dispensation of the law, it was the duty of the priestly tribe of the Levites to rise at dawn and give thanks and praise the Lord (1 Chronicles 23:30). We are not under the dispensation of the law, but as New Testament priests (1 Peter 2:5,9) we too should begin the day with God. If we do, we will have a keen sense of His presence with us throughout the busy hours that follow.

This great truth was obviously known by David. One of the most enjoyable verses to come from his pen is Psalm 143:8, "Cause me to hear Thy lovingkindness *in the morning;* for in Thee do I trust: cause me to know the way wherein I should walk; for I lift up my soul unto Thee." In this morning prayer David made two requests: to hear the lovingkindness of God in the morning; and to know the way in which he should walk throughout the day. These two requests bear a definite relationship.

David wanted the lovingkindness of God to engage his thoughts and affections early in the morning. If other thoughts get into our hearts in the morning, we may not be able to burn them away throughout the day. Prayer and praise, reading and meditation will influence our minds for hours throughout the day. Lovingkindness is a favorite theme of David. Simply, lovingkindness is love that shows kindness. By deeds and words it is God living through us to a hurting world. That's the kind of life David wanted to live. The Lord's lovingkindness is our all-sufficient source of joy. Such joy can be sought elsewhere but found only here. It is the divine joy that sweetens every bitter experience of life and makes even those that are sweet, sweeter still. It binds every wound, and is the balm for every hurt. It is little wonde that David sought such an experience early in the morning. With that kind of start, what must the rest of the day be like?

The old expression is here very applicable, "Well begun; half done." David began his day well by seeking the Lord and His lovingkindness. Half the battle of a successful day was already won. He continued to ask the Lord to show him the way he should walk throughout the day. Frequently the path we determine to be logical for our daily walk is not the path designed by God. We must keep the same close touch with Him hour after hour that we began with Him in the morning.

Speaking of his mountain-climbing experience, nineteenth century preacher George Barrell Cheever commented on this verse: "The whole valley is surrounded by ranges of regal crags, but the mountain, apparently absolutely inaccessible, is the last point which you would turn for an outlet. A side gorge that sweeps up to the glaciers and snowy pyramids flashing upon you in the opposite direction is the route which you suppose your guide is going to take. So convinced was I that the path must go in that direction, that I took a shortcut, which I conceived would bring me again into the mule path at a point under the glaciers; but after scaling precipices and getting lost in a wood of firs in the valley, I was glad to rejoin my friend with the guide, and to clamber on in pure ignorance and wonder."

We are tempted to walk our own way when we have no other resource. But as Christians we have a higher resource than our mind. We have the resource of the lovingkindness of God, which can be ours every morning if we but seek it. We should never attempt to walk alone throughout the day and to chart our own course when we have the ability to tap the resources of Heaven in the morning and receive our marching orders for the day, marching orders that are always designed to lead to victory. How foolish it is to neglect to seek the Lord in the morning and have to walk without Him the rest of the day.

MORNING HYMN

> *Thou my everlasting portion,*
> *More than friend or life to me;*
> *All along my pilgrim journey,*
> *Saviour, let me walk with Thee.*

Vengeance

MORNING SCRIPTURE   1 Samuel 25:1-38
MORNING VERSE   1 Samuel 25:36

And Abigail came to Nabal; and, behold, he held a feast in his house, like the feast of a king; and Nabal's heart was merry within him, for he was very drunken: wherefore she told him nothing, less or more, until the morning light.

ONE OF THE most obnoxious men in the Bible is Nabal. Nabal was a wealthy shepherd who had many flocks and servants. It appears that David and his men showed kindness to Nabal's servants and gave protection to them. Subsequently David's men needed provision and refreshment and he sent them to Nabal. But when David's men arrived at Carmel, Nabal lashed out at them, ridiculed them, and refused any help to them. The Bible describes Nabal as a churlish man "and evil in his doings." This simply means that he was hard to deal with, a difficult person to get along with. Not recognizing the anointing of God on David Nabal demanded, "Who is David? and who is the son of Jesse?" He ranked David among the common mavericks of the day. Nabal sent David's men away empty-handed. When the men returned to David and reported to him how offensively Nabal had acted and how unfriendly he had been, David's anger was piqued.

Four hundred of David's warriors were prepared to march against Nabal and retaliate for his unfriendly attitude. This would have engaged David in a sinful tirade against a sinful tyrant. Had it not been for the intervention of God through the actions of the quick-thinking wife of Nabal, David would undoubtedly have shed innocent blood that day. But Abigail, Nabal's wife, intercepted the irate David, brought gifts to him, and persuaded him not to take vengeance against her husband. She was God's messenger to God's man and David said to Abigail, "Blessed be the LORD God of Israel, which sent thee this day to meet me; and blessed be thy advice, and blessed be thou, which hast kept me this day from coming to shed blood, and from avenging myself with mine own hand." Nabal's attitude was unforgivable, but David's reaction was equally unforgivable. He would heed Abigail's advice, the same advice Paul gave to the Roman believers when he said, "Dearly beloved, avenge not yourselves, but rather give place unto [God's] wrath: for it is written, Vengeance is Mine; I will repay, saith the Lord" (Romans 12:19).

When Abigail returned to tell her husband what she had done, since he was filled with wine she wisely decided to tell him nothing *until the morning light* (1 Samuel 25:36). *In the morning* (verse 37), when Nabal was sober, Abigail related to him what she had done to spare his life and the reputation of David. At that point the churlish man apparently had a stroke and ten days later the Lord took his life. Abigail's wisdom permitted God to return the wickedness of Nabal upon his own head and still preserve David from making a foolish mistake.

General Robert E. Lee was asked what he thought of one of his fellow officers in the Confederate Army. This officer had made many derogatory remarks about General Lee. Lee rated him as a fine officer and good soldier. Someone questioned, saying, "General, I guess you don't know what he's been saying about you." Lee responded, "I know, but I was asked my opinion of him, not his opinion of me!"

Although we may be slandered or maligned by others we are not at liberty to do anything but show the love of the Lord Jesus unto them. Perhaps today you have an antagonist spreading falsehood about you. Do not plan to avenge the wrong you have been done; give place to God's wrath instead and speak kindly of that antagonist. Then and then alone will a difficult situation bring glory to the name of God.

MORNING HYMN

> *Open my eyes, that I may see*
> *Glimpses of truth Thou hast for me;*
> *Place in my hands the wonderful key*
> *That shall unclasp and set me free.*
> *Silently now I wait for Thee,*
> *Ready, my God, Thy will to see;*
> *Open my eyes—illumine me,*
> > *Spirit divine!*

Hospitality
and Inhospitality

MORNING SCRIPTURE   *Judges 19:1-30*
MORNING VERSE   *Judges 19:5*

And it came to pass on the fourth day, when they arose early in the morning, that he rose up to depart: and the damsel's father said unto his son-in-law, Comfort thine heart with a morsel of bread, and afterward go your way.

I N THE FAMILY LIFE of the ancient Near East, two important and contrasting features stand out in bold relief. They are the hospitality of the common folk and the inhospitality of those who are evil and cruel. The story of Judges 19 portrays both these features.

According to the historical account, a certain Levite who resided in the hill country of Ephraim took a concubine from Bethlehem-judah. Having proven unfaithful to him, the woman returned to her father's house in Bethlehem and there remained four months. After this separation the Levite decided to propose a reconciliation and thus traveled south to Bethlehem to speak with the woman and her father. Apparently the reconciliation was accomplished immediately for the father was quite happy to see his son-in-law.

The house of the Bethlehem father-in-law is a prime example of hospitality in the ancient Near East. Three days the son-in-law remained in the house and there "they did eat and drink." It was now time to leave. On the fourth day, *they arose early in the morning* in order to escape the punishing rays of the Palestinian sun (Judges 19:5). But the damsel's father invited his son-in-law to stay and have bread with him one more time. Soon the day had worn away and the invitation to tarry all night and wait for the morrow was given. Again the next day *he arose early in the morning* with the intent to leave, but the same thing happened (Judges 19:8). As the day wore on the man received a second invitation to tarry throughout the night, but this time he refused. With his wife he left Bethlehem and began to journey even though he knew he could not reach Mount Ephraim by nightfall.

Bypassing Jerusalem because the Jebusites lived there, the man chose to travel three miles further north to Gibeah where he anticipated a more hospitable reception. He found none and thus made preparations to spend the night in the street. Finally he and his wife were taken in by a former resident of Ephraim who now lived in Gibeah.

At this point the story begins to sound like Sodom and Gomorrah all over again. Base men, sons of Satan, encircled the house and began to beat on the door demanding that these men engage in a homosexual relationship with them. Perhaps taking his cue from Lot (cf. Genesis 19:1-11), unbelievably the master of the house offered his daughter and the Levite's concubine to the vicious mob in place of his house guest. This pacified the bisexual mob who abused the concubine all night long. When the Levite *rose up in the morning* and opened the doors of the house there he found the woman lying on the threshold (Judges 19:26-27).

Hospitality and inhospitality, both are seen here. What is it that causes one man to open his home in a gesture of hospitality and another man to beat down the door of a home to perform an act of homosexuality? What brings one man to do that which is delightful in the eyes of God and another to do that which is despicable in the eyes of God? Perhaps the answer is that we are made in the image of God and therefore have a desire to do good but have been marred by our own sin and have an innate bent toward evil. The Bethlehem father-in-law and the Ephraimite from Gibeah both sought to please others. The homosexual mob of Gibeah sought only to please themselves. Seeking one's own pleasure at the expense of all others arises out of a heart that is deceitful and desperately wicked (Jeremiah 17:9). There is no control over such a heart, only a cure found in the grace of salvation.

MORNING HYMN

> *Now incline me to repent,*
> *Let me now my sins lament;*
> *Now my foul revolt deplore,*
> *Weep, believe, and sin no more.*

Hidden Resources

MORNING SCRIPTURE   2 Samuel 23:1-17
MORNING VERSE   2 Samuel 23:4

And he shall be as the light of the morning, when the sun riseth, even a morning without clouds; as the tender grass springing out of the earth by clear shining after rain.

D AVID had returned to his capital city, Jerusalem. All serious challenges to his authority were now behind him. He was about to die at age seventy, having ruled Judah for seven years and as king over all Israel for another thirty-three years.

Indeed David was a very remarkable man. He had great ability, great insight, great grace. As a soldier, he was a mighty man of valor. As a poet, he was the "sweet psalmist of Israel." He was decisive in politics and chivalrous in war. But he was as human as he was great. Perhaps it's that quality about David that makes the man so lovable to us. David had boundless love for Jehovah and an unshakable faith and loyalty to Him. While he frequently stumbled and fell, he always knew how to get ahold of God, ask forgiveness, and go on for God. He had a true hunger to know the will of God and do it.

Second Samuel 23:1 claims to record the last words of David. Although these are the last literary or poetic words, David's final dying words are not recorded until 1 Kings 2. David describes the kind of man God would have as king of Israel. "He that ruleth over men must be just" (2 Samuel 23:3). One who would be king, president, prime minister, or any leader can never assume he or she possesses the qualifications for these important tasks unless that person has a sense of justice that is more than human. Human justice views all men as created equal. Divine justice views all men as created equal before God, a God with whom all men have to do. This is why the next clause is so important. A godly leader is one "ruling in the fear of God."

When Jethro counseled Moses about organizing Israel he said, "Moreover thou shalt provide out of all the people able men, such as fear God, men of truth, hating covetousness; and place such over them to be rulers of thousands, and rulers of hundreds, rulers of fifties, and rulers of tens" (Exodus 18:21). As important as it is that a ruler be just, the capability to be just arises only out of a fear of God. God would have no one rule Israel who did not fear Him.

How can we draw upon the resource of the fear of God in order to be just to all men? We must depend upon our hidden resources. All nature depends on hidden resources. Rivers, deep and wide, have their sources in the snowcapped mountains. Great trees are only as strong as the part you cannot see, their root system. The entire earth draws upon the water and minerals under the ground, their hidden resources. A ruler in America, in Israel, anywhere in the world, will only be as great as his fear of God, and his fear of God will only be as deep as his hidden resources in God. This is why choosing a nation's leader must go beyond partisan politics, beyond basic morality, beyond simple decency.

David was keenly aware that he had not always exhibited the fear of God, the kind of fear that is pure, pristine, and clear. He describes the just man who fears God as one who "shall be as the *light of the morning,* when the sun riseth, *even a morning* without clouds" (2 Samuel 23:4). This kind of clearness and brightness comes only to a man who seeks the Lord, his hidden resource, early in the morning before he begins to make the decisions of his day. Let's pray that God will give us that kind of ruler.

MORNING HYMN

> *Take time to be holy,*
> *Speak oft with thy Lord;*
> *Abide in Him always*
> *And feed on His Word.*
> *Make friends of God's children,*
> *Help those who are weak,*
> *Forgetting in nothing*
> *His blessing to seek.*

God's Providence

MORNING SCRIPTURE   1 Samuel 29:1-11
MORNING VERSE   1 Samuel 29:10

Wherefore now rise up early in the morning with thy master's servants that are come with thee: and as soon as ye be up early in the morning, and have light, depart.

WHEN we live lives that are pleasing before the Lord, godly lives, righteous lives, we may always be assured that no matter where our steps take us, we have been led there by the Lord God Himself. Indeed, "The steps of a good man are ordered by the LORD" (Psalm 37:23).

By this time in his life the madness of King Saul had become so notable that he nearly destroyed himself and his nation as well. His hatred for David and his jealousy of this young Bethlehemite caused David to be resigned to a life of wandering. Once David learned that the Philistines were besieging the city of Keilah, he immediately hurried to rescue the city. Successful in his rescue, he drove off the enemy and scattered them, making this for a short time his headquarters (1 Samuel 23:1-6). However, whenever Saul learned of the whereabouts of David he was sure to be persistent in his pursuit of him and again David was forced to flee (1 Samuel 23:7-14). Although during his wanderings David attracted to his side six hundred soldiers in support of his cause, nevertheless these were days of hardship and grief for David. Finally he had to leave the kingdom entirely and seek refuge among his former enemies, the Philistines.

Although the enemy clearly remembered that David slew the giant Goliath, now he was an enemy of Israel's king and so the Philistines made an unlikely alliance with David and his men. With the consent of Achish, king of Gath, David made his headquarters at Ziklag for more than a year (1 Samuel 27:1-7). Because he supported the Philistine king in raids on the tribes to the south of the wilderness of Shur (1 Samuel 27:8-12), David gained the respect and friendship of Achish. Things were fine as long as the Philistines were fighting someone other than the Israelites. But that situation was about to change.

The Philistine armies assembled at Aphek to encounter the

Israelites in Jezreel. David was now in a desperately ticklish situation. He was with the armies of the Philistines, arrayed in preparation for battle against his own people, Israel. What would he do? How would God get him out of this jam?

David didn't have to wait long for a resolution to the problem. The princes of the Philistines began to wonder whether or not they could trust David fighting against his own people. If he were to win the favor of King Saul again, what better way than to kill the Philistines. Therefore Achish commanded, "Wherefore now *rise up early in the morning* with thy master's servants that are come with thee: and as soon as ye be *up early in the morning*, and have light, depart" (1 Samuel 29:10). Once again, through the suspicions of the Philistines, God had spared David from fighting against his own people.

Rowland V. Bingham, founder of the Sudan Interior Mission, was once seriously injured in a terrible automobile accident. Rushed to the hospital in critical condition, he did not regain consciousness until the next day. When he asked the nurse what he was doing there, she replied, "Don't try to talk now, just rest. You have been in an accident." "Accident? Accident?" exclaimed Dr. Bingham. "There are no accidents in the life of the Christian. This is just an incident in God's perfect leading." Our attitude toward the Lord's leading our steps ought to be the same. When we live righteously before Him, free from known sin, there are no accidents in our lives, only incidents in His perfect leading. Let Him lead you today.

MORNING HYMN

In shady, green pastures, so rich and so sweet,
    God leads His dear children along;
Where the water's cool flow bathes the weary one's feet,
    God leads His dear children along.
Some thru the waters, some thru the flood,
Some thru the fire, but all thru the blood;
Some thru great sorrow, but God gives a song,
In the night season and all the day long.

Morning Praise

MORNING SCRIPTURE   Psalm 113:1-9
MORNING VERSE   Psalm 113:3

From the rising of the sun unto the going down of the same the LORD's name is to be praised.

L IKE the two psalms preceding it this one is without title. Some commentators have ascribed it to Samuel, others to David. However the authorship is unknown. Whoever the author was, in his best journalistic style he answers the five key questions that any young reporter would ask when writing a story: he answers the five W's: who, what, when, where, and why. Let's notice what has excited this young reporter to write in such a way.

Who. To whom does the writer speak? To all of us. Anyone who reads this psalm is included in the "ye" of verse 1, most specifically, "O ye servants of the LORD." More than anyone else, the servants of the Lord ought to be involved in the exalted activity of praising God. Each of us who claims to serve the Lord must publicly discharge our responsibility. We are best acquainted with the reasons for praising Him and we are also the best instruments to declare His praise.

What. The responsibility of the servants of the Lord is simply, "Praise ye the LORD . . . praise the name of the LORD." The repetition of this phrase in a single verse is not without significance. You would think that we who have been saved by His grace would automatically and consistently praise His name. However this is not the case, for we are frequently slow in praising God for His blessings. Therefore the psalmist finds it necessary to stimulate us, to cajole us, and the repetition of the stimulus calls us to perseverance in sounding forth the praises of God.

When. To indicate when the servants of the Lord are to be engaged in praising the Lord the psalmist uses an expression which is more characteristic of the old Greek poets than of the Hebrew prophets. He says, *"From the rising of the sun* unto the going down of the same the LORD's name is to be praised" (Psalm 113:3). This poetic expression indicates that there is never a time of the day, never a waking hour, never an inappropriate moment, when the servant of the Lord cannot praise His name. We are to begin His praise at the very rising of the sun, early in the morning, and to continue that praise until sunset. Praising the name of the Lord is a daylong, lifelong privilege.

Where. If we are to praise the Lord from the rising of the sun until the going down of the same, where is it we shall engage in this exalted activity? Since "the LORD is high above all nations, and His glory above heaven," and yet He "humbleth himself to behold the things that are in heaven, and in the earth," it is incumbent upon us to see that His name is praised wherever His presence is known. Therefore we are to praise His name in the highest heavens and the lowest earth. Just as there is not a waking hour that is inappropriate to praise His name, there is not the slightest place on earth that is inappropriate to the praising of His name. As servants of the Lord, we are to praise Him continually, wherever we find ourselves.

Why. The reasons for praising the Lord are manifold. He is high above all nations, and His glory above the heavens. Still he humbleth Himself to observe our affairs on earth. He raiseth the poor out of the dust and the needy out of the dunghill. He makes princes out of paupers and makes the barren woman a homemaker and the mother of children.

Today would be a good day for us to make a praise list. Just as we have a prayer list, Christians ought to have a praise list, a list of reasons for praising the Lord. Begin with His love for you, His death for you, and His salvation of you, and keep listing things for which to praise the Lord from morning to night. Don't be surprised if you have to make a second list for we have much for which to praise the Lord. A praise list—it's an idea worth consideration.

MORNING HYMN

> *O for a thousand tongues to sing*
> *My great Redeemer's praise,*
> *The glories of my God and King,*
> *The triumphs of His grace.*

He Is Alive

MORNING SCRIPTURE   Mark 16:1-20
MORNING VERSE   Mark 16:9

Now when Jesus was risen early the first day of the week, He appeared first to Mary Magdalene, out of whom He had cast seven devils.

PERHAPS the most astounding event ever to take place early in the morning occurred on the first Easter morning. God is in the habit of doing things early in the morning but on this particular morning He did something very special. He raised Jesus Christ from the dead and the mighty power of God was proved by the post-resurrection appearances of our Lord.

In Mark 16 three such appearances of the risen Saviour are recorded. Verse 14 indicates that "He appeared unto the eleven as they sat at meat." The disciples had assembled themselves, except Thomas, and were not given to believing the reports that Jesus was alive. Suddenly He appeared in their midst, the doors of the room being shut, and they perceived Him to be a spirit. But He called unto them to feel His body, He showed them the wounds in His hands, His feet, and His side. As some still doubted, He ate food before them all. He rebuked them for their lack of faith. But He also commissioned them to "Go ye into all the world, and preach the gospel to every creature" (verse 15). This was the last of His appearances on that great resurrection day.

Prior to this occasion, however, He appeared to two individuals walking on the road to Emmaus. Although only briefly mentioned by Mark, the interesting narrative given by Luke tells us that Cleopas and another had left the city after visiting the sepulcher and were on their way to the village of Emmaus, some seven miles from Jerusalem. As they were engaged in conversation, Jesus Himself joined them. They invited Him to accompany them to the home of Cleopas; they did not recognize Him as the risen Lord. Suddenly, "And beginning at Moses and all the prophets, he expounded unto them in all the scriptures the things concerning himself" (Luke 24:27). Still, when they reported to the others that they had met the risen Lord, the disciples found that difficult to believe.

But to whom was the first postresurrection appearance made? Did Jesus first appear to Peter, the principal preacher of Christianity in the first century? Did He appear to John, the beloved disciple, the disciple whom Jesus loved? No, He appeared to one whose devotion to Him could not be excelled. He appeared to one whose dedication to Him could not be surpassed. He appeared first to one who was an unlikely candidate for such an honor. Mark 16:9 says, "Now when Jesus was risen *early the first day of the week* He appeared first to Mary Magdalene, out of whom He had cast seven devils." Yes, Mary Magdalene would be the first one to see the risen Lord even though she was not an apostle nor would she ever be used of God to write a single line of Scripture. Her only qualification for this high honor was her deep and abiding affection for her Lord.

The Gospel of Luke records that when Jesus was preaching in every city and village, the twelve disciples being with Him, a company of women followed them. This occurred out of sheer gratitude for what the Lord had done in their behalf. One of them was Mary called Magdalene, out of whom Jesus cast seven devils. From the moment of her exorcism by the Lord Jesus, Mary followed her Master and the disciple band and ministered unto Him, as did the other women, of their substance (Luke 8:1-3). This unremitting devotion was the quality found by the Lord to be the most rewardable of all.

It is not as important what we bring to the service of the Lord as it is how much we love the Lord we serve. Mary would never be used as the disciples would; she would never be recorded as one of the great leaders of the first century Church. Still, Jesus first appeared to Mary Magdalene after His resurrection because she, in absolute devotion to her Master, was keeping a vigil outside the tomb after she had reported to Peter and John that Jesus of Nazareth was risen. Oh that our devotion to the Lord would parallel that of this simple woman. How much we love Him is far more important than how much we serve Him.

MORNING HYMN

> *Risen for me, risen for me,*
> *Up from the grave He has risen for me;*
> *Now evermore from death's sting I am free,*
> *All because Jesus has risen for me.*

Pride

MORNING SCRIPTURE   2 Samuel 24:1-25
MORNING VERSE   2 Samuel 24:11

For when David was up in the morning, the word of the LORD came unto the prophet Gad, David's seer.

HAVE YOU ever noticed that you make your greatest mistakes immediately after your greatest victories? Why is that? The answer is likely pride. The Bible frequently warns us about the penalty of pride. Proverbs 16:18 says, "Pride goeth before destruction, and an haughty spirit before a fall." The pages of the Holy Scriptures are filled with people who have met their defeat, not because of their inferiority, but because of their haughty and arrogant spirit.

A graphic illustration of the penalty of pride is seen in the life of King David. A man after God's own heart, David early won favor with Jehovah for his faithfulness and purity of life. He rose above the usurpation of his throne by two of his sons. He lived down the shame of his sin with Bathsheba. Now he had come to the end of his life, a valiant warrior and a victor.

Following the catalog of David's mighty men is the statement, "And again the anger of the LORD was kindled against Israel, and he moved David against them to say, Go, number Israel and Judah" (2 Samuel 24:1). The wrath of God was upon His people at this time not so much for a specific offense as for the general deterioration of their faithfulness to Him. First Chronicles 21:1 indicates that it was Satan who incited David to take this census. Although the penalty for this sin affected all people, David accepted it as the result of his own personal sin. Why? Because the numbering of the people was done in pride, for the purpose of self-glory, and pride always pays a penalty.

Immediately after David learned the strength of his army, he recognized the basis for his need to know their number. "And David said unto the LORD, I have sinned greatly in that I have done . . . for I have done very foolishly." As soon as David was *up in the morning* (2 Samuel 24:11), God offered three potential punishments for this pride. David's options were not good: the people could endure seven years of famine; David could fle three months from his enemies; Israel could experience three days of the worst pestilence they had ever seen. David preferred to receive punishment from God rather than from his enemies. Thus the Lord sent a pestilence upon Israel in the morning. Because of Israel's continued sin and David's pride, seventy thousand men died during the next three days in Israel.

There is an old fable about two ducks and a frog that played together in a small pond. Each summer, when the days got long and hot, the pond shrank to a small puddle and the ducks and frog were forced to move. The ducks could fly to another place, but not the frog. As the fable goes, the frog finally suggested that the ducks put a stick in their bills so he could cling to it with his mouth and thus fly away with them. The frog was very proud of his brilliant idea. As the ducks took off for a nearby lake, the stick between their bills and the frog clinging tightly, they passed over a farmer who seeing this strange sight questioned, "Well, isn't that a clever stunt! I wonder who thought of it?" Swelling with pride, the frog said, "I did!" and with that he lost his grip and went crashing to the ground. His own pride had done him in.

Let us beware of our pride today, for it may lead to the same kind of painful end that the frog experienced. Even worse, it may lead to pain inflicted upon others, as was experienced in the life of David. Remember, "Pride goeth before destruction" (Proverbs 16:18).

MORNING HYMN

> *Lord Jesus, look down from Thy throne in the skies*
> *And help me to make a complete sacrifice.*
> *I give up myself and whatever I know—*
> *Now wash me and I shall be whiter than snow*

Relying on God

MORNING SCRIPTURE   Psalm 127:1-5
MORNING VERSE   Psalm 127:2

It is vain for you to rise up early, to sit up late, to eat the bread of sorrows: for so He giveth His beloved sleep.

THE THEME of this delightful little psalm is the folly of human effort apart from God. Anything we attempt in life is doomed to failure unless we rely on the power of God. The psalmist shows us this is true in four aspects of human life: social (verse 1a); civic (verse 1b); business (verse 2); and domestic (verses 3-5). In each of these there is an unmistakable emphasis on the necessity for reliance on God.

"Except the LORD build the house, they labour in vain that build it." Regardless if it is a private dwelling or the house of God, it is useless to undertake building unless we seek the prosperity of God. The psalmist does not say that unless the Lord consents that the house should be built, he says unless the Lord *builds* the house. We supply the materials; He does the work in our social lives.

"Except the LORD keep the city, the watchman waketh but in vain." Turning from social to civic life, the psalmist knows the unseen watchman of every city is Jehovah Himself. The constant vigilance of a sentinel is without reward if he watches alone. It does little good for us to stand watch unless the Lord stands with us. Not to set a watch when the enemy is at hand is foolish, but to set a watch in our own strength is just as foolish.

"It is vain for you *to rise up early*, to sit up late, to eat the bread of sorrows." Here the psalmist does not counsel us against rising early. His intent is to show us that nothing is accomplished by rising early or staying up late if all we do is fret about our problems. Here too we must have absolute dependence upon God.

Finally, the psalmist turns his attention to reliance on God in domestic matters. He begins with a statement about children which is diametrically opposed to the philosophy of the world today. In a day in which children are frequently viewed as a bother, an infringement on personal freedom, and are therefore aborted before they are born, the psalmist counters, "Lo, children are an heritage of the LORD." Children come to us from God and are another means of building a house. In fact, in the Hebrew, the word for son (*ben*) and daughter (*bath*) both come from the same root word for house (*beth*). Although building a house is akin to building sons and daughters, building sons and daughters is more important than building a house around them.

A preacher once was entertained by a couple who had two teenage boys. When he entered the house he noticed immediately a sense of warmth. He also noticed that the living room carpet was very tattered. Before he left, the mother related that one day several boys from the neighborhood were having a good time in her living room. Perhaps they were being a little too rough and she asked them to play elsewhere. They responded, "But where will we go?" Nodding to one of them she asked, "How about your place?" "Not a chance," replied the boy. "We're not allowed to invite kids into our house." Others questioned gave similar replies. The mother soon sensed that her home was the only one where the boys felt free to come and have fun. From then on they were always welcome.

While the mother did not allow the children to be disrespectful to her property, she nonetheless recognized that the rug was only property, but that children were an heritage from the Lord. She knew if she were to raise a family she would have to show a lot of love and rely on the Lord.

To whatever endeavor God calls you today, whether it be social, civic, business, or domestic, reliance on Him is a prerequisite to success. You cannot build a house fruitfully without the labor of God. You cannot watch a city successfully without the protection of God. You cannot engage in business tirelessly without the strength of God. You cannot raise children lovingly without the wisdom of God. All human activity is but folly unless you rely upon God for success. Ask Him to make you successful today.

MORNING HYMN

> *If God build not the house, and lay*
> *The groundwork sure—whoever build,*
> *It cannot stand one stormy day.*
> *If God be not the city's shield,*
> *If He be not their bars and wall,*
> *In vain is watchtower, men, and all.*

Jesus First

MORNING SCRIPTURE   *Revelation 22:1-21*
MORNING VERSE   *Revelation 22:16*

*I Jesus have sent mine angel to testify unto you these things in
the churches. I am the root and the offspring of David, and the
bright and morning star.*

JUST AS Genesis, the first book of the Bible, is a book of beginnings, Revelation, the last book of the Bible, is a book of new
beginnings. Before these new beginnings can occur, however,
a series of endings must transpire. Thus the book of Revelation
represents numerous "finals" in the Word of God.

Genesis 3:9 is God's initial call to man: "And the LORD God
called unto Adam, and said unto him, Where art thou?" Revelation 22:17 is God's final call to man: "And the Spirit and the bride
say, come. And let him that heareth say, Come. And let him that is
athirst come. And whosoever will, let him take the water of life
freely." Somewhere between Genesis 3:9 and Revelation 22:17
everyone who would enjoy eternity in Heaven with Christ must
answer one of God's calls. Perhaps you have answered Jesus' call
in Matthew 11:28, "Come unto Me, all ye that labour and are
heavy laden, and I will give you rest." Or maybe it was the call of
Christ in John 4:14, "But whosoever drinketh of the water that I
shall give him shall never thirst; but the water that I shall give
him shall be in him a well of water springing up into everlasting
life." But if you have not responded to the call of Christ, if you
have never received Jesus Christ as your Saviour, you must re-
spond to His call in order to receive eternal life.

Once we have responded positively to the Lord's call to
salvation, we have a whole new outlook on the future. Our
destiny is brighter. Our lives are sunnier. The birds' songs are
sweeter. We look forward to serving Jesus every day and antici-
pate the day we shall live with Him in glory.

Just before God's final call in Revelation 22:17, Jesus verifies
that He is indeed the one to whom we are called in salvation. He
says, "I am the root and the offspring of David, and the *bright and
morning star*" (Revelation 22:16). These titles are applied to Him
elsewhere in Scripture (cf. Isaiah 11:1; Numbers 24:17), but no-

where do they take on more meaning than just prior to the final call in the Bible. When we come to God in salvation, we come to the offspring of David. When we leave the darkness of sin, we enter the light of the Bright and Morning Star. It is the shining face of Jesus, the one who died for us, that we will first want to see when we enter the brightness of Heaven. After all, being with our Saviour is what makes Heaven heavenly.

When Fanny Crosby, the hymn writer who wrote more than eight thousand gospel songs even though she was blinded at the age of six weeks, was pitied by a friend because she could not see, Miss Crosby replied, "Do you know that if at birth I had been able to make one petition, it would have been that I would have been born blind?" The friend was puzzled by this answer and asked her for further explanation. "Because when I get to Heaven, the first face that shall ever gladden my sight will be that of my Saviour!" We too will want to see our Saviour first of all.

There is a story about Cyrus, the founder of the Persian Empire, who once captured a prince and his entire family. When they came before the monarch, Cyrus asked the prisoner, "What will you give me if I release you?" The prince replied, "The half of my wealth." "And if I release your children?" Again the prince replied, "Everything I possess." Finally Cyrus said, "And what will you give me if I will release your wife?" The prince replied, "Your Majesty, I will give myself." So moved was Cyrus by the devotion of this young prince that he freed him and his entire family. As the prince, his wife, and children returned to their home, the prince said to his wife, "Wasn't Cyrus a handsome man!" With a tender look of love in her eyes, the wife said to her husband, "I did not notice. I could only keep my eyes on you—the one who was willing to give himself for me."

Morning by morning we arise to give praise to the one who saved us. Day by day we serve the one who saved us. Evening by evening we rejoice in the one who saved us. Let's concentrate today on loving the Lord Jesus and adoring no other face than the one who loved us so much that He died for us (John 3:16).

MORNING HYMN

> *All hail the pow'r of Jesus' name!*
> *Let angels prostrate fall;*
> *Bring forth the royal diadem,*
> *And crown Him Lord of all.*

Standing Tall

MORNING SCRIPTURE   Job 1:1-22
MORNING VERSE   Job 1:5

And it was so, when the days of their feasting were gone about, that Job sent and sanctified them, and rose up early in the morning, and offered burnt offerings according to the number of them all: for Job said, It may be that my sons have sinned, and cursed God in their hearts. Thus did Job continually.

T HE ABILITY to meet affliction with an uncompromising endurance and an unflinching respect for God is one of the marks of true Christian character. Certainly Job is the classic example of a man who met affliction in such a way.

The author begins the book of Job by describing a beautiful pastoral scene in which Job, a respected and honored oriental sheik or prince, was residing in the land of Uz. Job was a man of extreme wealth possessing a flock of seven thousand sheep, three thousand camels, large tracts of land, and an affectionate family of seven sons and three daughters.

But more than this, Job was a man of extreme piety. The first verse of the book describes him as "perfect and upright, and one that feared God, and eschewed evil." So concerned was this man about keeping himself and his family right before his God that he *"rose up early in the morning,* and offered burnt offerings according to the number of them all; for Job said, It may be that my sons have sinned, and cursed God in their hearts. Thus did Job continually" (Job 1:5). Day after day he met God early, bringing sacrifices to the Almighty in the event that he or any of his family had secretly sinned against God.

The rest of this chapter's verses, comprising scene two in the first act of Job's life, read like a horror story. Here Satan entered this beautiful country scene and disrupted the simple pastoral life of Job and his family. Notice these features of scene two.

1. *Satan's report* (verse 6). The day came when the sons of God, presumably the angels, were to bring a report of their activities to Jehovah. Satan also came among them.

2. *Satan's activity* (verse 7). When Jehovah asked Satan why he had come and from where he had come, Lucifer answered the

Lord, "From going to and fro in the earth, and from walking up and down in it." Satan's activity was a never-ending search for opportunities to disrupt the program of God.

3. *Satan's problem* (verse 8). It was Jehovah who suggested to Satan, "Hast thou considered My servant Job?" Here Satan would encounter a man who was perfect and upright, one who hated every kind of evil that Satan had placed in his path.

4. *Satan's accusation* (verses 10-11). The devil had a ready answer for why Job had remained upright. God had put a hedge around him so that everything Job did prospered. Surely if God would remove that hedge, Satan reasoned, Job certainly would curse God to His face.

5. *Satan's restriction* (verse 12). Jehovah permitted Lucifer to touch all that Job possessed but placed one restriction upon him, "Only upon himself put not forth thine hand." Although God does not always make this temporal restriction with regard to us today, he certainly makes it an eternal restriction.

6. *Satan's attacks* (verses 13-19). The devil came to menace Job. Like waves of enemy soldiers the reports kept coming to Job until he learned that he had lost all.

7. *Satan's failure* (verses 20-22). Job arose and reacted with characteristic remorse. And yet, rather than sin and foolishly charge God, Job stood tall and simply stated, "Naked came I out of my mother's womb, and naked shall I return thither: the LORD gave and the LORD hath taken away; blessed be the name of the LORD" (Job 1:21).

Do not be discouraged when you face the attacks of the wicked one. These attacks are only temporal and our loving God will have the final word. You may not always understand the ways of God, but you must always trust them, as did Job.

MORNING HYMN

> *Why should I feel discouraged,*
> *Why should the shadows come,*
> *Why should my heart be lonely*
> *And long for Heav'n and home,*
> *When Jesus is my portion?*
> *My constant Friend is He;*
> *His eye is on the sparrow,*
> *And I know He watches me.*

Ingredients for Service

MORNING SCRIPTURE   Exodus 34:1-35
MORNING VERSE   Exodus 34:2

And be ready in the morning, and come up in the morning unto mount Sinai, and present thyself there to Me in the top of the mount.

T HE MAN who bows the lowest in the presence of God stands the straightest in the presence of sin. If this truth was known by anyone in the Old Testament, it was known by Moses. Time after time he had to stand straight and tall in the face of Israel's sin. Once even while Moses was communing with God on the top of Sinai, Israel was brewing a pot of sin. Upon his descent from the mount, viewing the golden calf and licentious behavior of Israel, Moses' righteous indignation caused him to cast the tables of God's Law to the ground, crushing them to pieces (Exodus 32:19). The people were rebuked for their sin, three thousand men were capitally punished, Moses interceded for the lives of the rest, and the golden calf crisis was over.

But there would be more sin and the tables of stone had to be replaced. Thus the Lord issued Moses another summons to Sinai with these instructions: "And be ready *in the morning*, and come up *in the morning* unto mount Sinai, and present thyself there to Me in the top of the mount" (Exodus 34:2). Note the words, "be ready," "come up," and "present thyself." Moses' renewed call to service contained these three essential ingredients found in every call to service God issues.

Be ready. The man God uses is the man who is ready, willing, and able to be used. If we are not ready, God will bypass us for someone who is, ahd we will miss the blessing that could have been ours. The Apostle Paul was a man who was ready. In Romans 1:15 he was "ready to preach the gospel to you that are at Rome also." With Paul preaching was a passion: "For I am ready not to be bound only, but also to die at Jerusalem for the name of the Lord Jesus" (Acts 21:13). After a long life of service to his Lord, Paul exclaimed, "For I am now ready to be offered, and the time of my departure is at hand. I have fought a good fight, I have finished my course, I have kept the faith" (2 Timothy 4:6-7)

Paul was ready to preach, ready to suffer, even ready to die in the service of the Lord.

Come up. We cannot be of service to God until we first come to Him in salvation. But Jehovah's call to Moses was not to salvation but to communion and service. Once the Lord has called us to be saved, He then calls us to "come and dine" (John 21:12). In other words, as Moses, we are called to fellowship with the Lord. We "come up" to the Lord God in prayer. Like salvation, prayer and communion with God precede service (Ephesians 6:18-20).

Present thyself. The final ingredient in preparing for service to God and standing in the face of sin is to present ourselves to Him. Paul begged the Roman believers to "present your bodies a living sacrifice, holy, acceptable unto God, which is your reasonable service" (Romans 12:1). Being ready to serve God is necessary. Coming up to God in prayer is likewise necessary in preparing for useful service. But unless we are willing to present ourselves to God—body, mind, and soul—as Moses did, there is little chance that He will use us or that we will successfully stand straight and tall in the presence of sin.

When the call of God came, Moses prepared a second pair of stone tablets for the law of God and *"rose up early in the morning,* and went up unto Mount Sinai, as the LORD had commanded him" (Exodus 34:4). Moses was ready for service, early in the morning, for he knew that there was a lot of sin yet to be dealt with in the camp of Israel. Moses must stand straight and tall in the presence of that sin, as each believer must. Are you ready to rise early each morning and come to God in prayer, presenting yourself in service to Him? Your day will go much better if you are.

MORNING HYMN

> *Stand up, stand up for Jesus,*
> > *Ye soldiers of the cross;*
> *Lift high His royal banner,*
> > *It must not suffer loss:*
> *From vict'ry unto vict'ry*
> > *His army shall He lead,*
> *Till ev'ry foe is vanquished,*
> > *And Christ is Lord indeed.*

The Hidden Hammer

MORNING SCRIPTURE   Job 7:1-21
MORNING VERSE   Job 7:21

*And why dost thou not pardon my transgression, and take away
mine iniquity? for now shall I sleep in the dust; and thou shalt
seek me in the morning, but I shall not be.*

T HE BOTTOM had fallen out of Job's life. All his possessions
had been destroyed. His family had been slaughtered, and
any hope for a posterity was gone. God had delivered Job
into Satan's hand. Those associated with Job could not understand why this had happened. Even his wife counseled him to
"curse God and die" (Job 2:9). But Job was fully convinced that if
God had permitted this evil to come to him the evil would
ultimately turn to good.

Job's friend Eliphaz expressed surprise that Job, who in the
past comforted others, was now giving way to sorrow. His friend
wrongly judged that if Job had nothing to be ashamed of, he had
no reason to be sorrowful. Theologically he understood misfor-
tune always to be the result of sin. Therefore there was no other
explanation than that Job had sinned and the route of escape was
not a bitter complaint but a bold confession of sin to receive the
fruit of blessing. Understandably Job was offended at the speech
of his friend. Eliphaz had magnified Job's complaint and mini-
mized his condition. Just think of it. Life had collapsed around
him and Job could think of no specific cause for that. He knew
Eliphaz was wrong in his assessment of the situation.

In chapter 7 Job is philosophical about the brevity of life. He
knows that the days of man upon the earth are numbered. He
likens them to the cloud that is consumed and vanishes away.
Since life is so brief and his life is now so filled with anguish,
why does Jehovah even bother with Job? Why does He reveal
Himself to Job *every morning* and try him every moment (Job
7:18)? In his condition, life is worth less than death and Job
desires that "thou shalt seek me *in the morning*, but I shall not be"
(Job 7:21). The blows that God permitted Satan to land on Job
appear to have been merciless. His life had been upright and just.
How could God allow this to happen?

Samuel Chadwick relates that when he was a boy he often went to the local blacksmith shop to watch the smithy work. He remembers how the smith would take a large piece of iron and place it in the fire with tongs and then work the bellows to make it white-hot. Then after removing the piece of iron from the fire and laying it upon the anvil, he would take a small hammer and begin to tap on the iron. No sooner would the smith tap the iron with the small hammer than a big man on the other side of the anvil would come crashing down hard with a large sledge hammer, hitting the iron on the exact same spot that the blacksmith had just tapped. Inquisitively, Chadwick once commented to the blacksmith, "You don't do much good with that little hammer, do you?" The gentle blacksmith laughed and replied, "No, my boy, but I show that big fellow where to place the blow."

When the bottom fell out of Job's life and his friends came to comfort him, none of them was aware of all that had transpired in Heaven before these calamities began. None of them knew that God had given Satan permission to afflict Job. They were totally unaware that while Satan was pounding away at Job with his unholy sledge hammer, each blow was being carefully guided by a loving Heavenly Father. God would show Satan where he could deliver his blows on Job, just like the blacksmith defined for his large friend where he could hit the iron with his sledge hammer.

If you are today experiencing unjust criticism, undue persecution, or unreturned love, please remember that as a child of God Satan can never afflict you beyond that which God, your loving Heavenly Father, gives him permission to do. God is still in control and though friends may unrighteously condemn us, as long as we live a life clean before Him, we need not be concerned about what Satan can do to us.

MORNING HYMN

> *Day by day and with each passing moment,*
> *Strength I find to meet my trials here;*
> *Trusting in my Father's wise bestowment,*
> *I've no cause for worry or for fear,*
> *He whose heart is kind beyond all measure*
> *Gives unto each day what He deems best,*
> *Lovingly, its part of pain and pleasure,*
> *Mingling toil with peace and rest.*

Early in the Morning

Early in the morning
> I rise to meet the Lord,
He makes His presence known to me
> Through the pages of His Word.

For when I meet Him early
> At the dawning of the day,
The hours go more smoothly
> Whatever comes my way.

But if I fail to meet Him
> And rush to other things,
I face the kind of failures
> That a day without Him brings.

So here's a little secret
> To make your day go right,
Meet God early in the morning
> And praise Him every night.

KROLL